NEW HAMPSHIRE
BOOK
OF THE
DEAD

NEW HAMPSHIRE
BOOK
OF THE
DEAD

GRAVEYARD LEGENDS
AND LORE

Roxie J. Zwicker

THE
History
PRESS

Published by The History Press
Charleston, SC 29403
www.historypress.net

First published 2012

Manufactured in the United States

ISBN 978.1.60949.756.9

Library of Congress CIP data applied for.

Contents

Introduction

Let's talk of graves, of worms, and epitaphs.
—William Shakespeare, Richard II

I have always found cemeteries to be fascinating, and I've made many efforts to find them on my travels throughout New Hampshire. If I was traveling along the seacoast in the summer or driving through the Great North Woods in the winter and there was a cemetery nearby, I would stop and take a look. Often, I would find something unusual while exploring these cemeteries that would arouse my curiosity. Unusual carvings and epitaphs have always attracted my attention, and the cemeteries of New Hampshire have never disappointed me. I have often read inscriptions on gravestones out loud while in the cemetery, sometimes having to sound out words to decipher the old spelling. A few times, I have gently reached out to lightly touch the lettering as I read, imagining how the stone carver carved each line. Some stones have called to me, beckoning me to not only stop and cast an eye on them but also to sit quietly in front of them and contemplate the life of the deceased. I'm sure the townsfolk and pioneers buried here never imagined that an unrelated stranger might one day visit their graves.

I've always felt it was my duty to pay respects to those who have gone before, regardless of whether I knew them or not. I often hope that just the mention of someone's name on a gravestone helps bring him or her back to life for at least a moment and that he or she is not forgotten, even though his or her gravestone may be moldering deep in the woods of New Hampshire. The events and experiences that these people had in America's early history paved the way for people like you and me to live our lives the way we do, free from oppression and in a civilized society that is quite different from life in past centuries.

How do we learn the story of those who came before us, and how do we pay our respects? Simply visiting a cemetery, stopping to read a gravestone, placing a flag on a veteran's grave—these actions connect us to our past. But words chiseled into stones that crumble year by year continue to fade, and our past is becoming ever more distant.

There is no better place to connect with our history than in a cemetery. Many people I've spoken with are rather superstitious about visiting cemeteries because it causes them to face the grim reality of the inevitable: death. I often wonder if they have ever thought that a cemetery visit could help inspire life. The epitaphs on the gravestones tell us that we are living in a country that many struggled, fought and died for.

Some people are drawn to cemeteries, wanting to connect with the ghosts that might linger there, and New Hampshire is not lacking in haunted burial places; there is one in every corner of the state. Perhaps the spirits there are trying to link the present with the past to remind us of their story, show us how connected we truly are and how they should not be forgotten.

The intention of this book is to tell some of the tales of New Hampshire's deceased, from the settlers who first stepped on the sandy beaches of the coast to those that dwelled in the mountains and lived off the land.

There are many stories tucked away in the state's cemeteries. I hope you enjoy the ones included in this book.

Chapter One

Discovering Historic New Hampshire Graveyards

The still North remembers them,
The hill-winds know their name,
And the granite of New Hampshire
Keeps the record of their fame

—Alma Mater, Dartmouth College

There is something about roaming New Hampshire's back roads that sets the imagination wandering. The picturesque barns and quaint family farms dot the rolling foothills in the southwestern part of the state. Roads lead into the woods, and there are places where you may not see another vehicle or human face for miles. The majesty of the White Mountains is nothing less than awe-inspiring, with an allure that has been calling naturalists and vacationers for hundreds of years. The towering cliffs and mountain ridges lined with pine trees invite explorers to find the paths that Native Americans once walked. New Hampshire is also proud of its scenic (albeit tiny) seacoast, where visitors from Europe visited the shores as early as the sixteenth century. Here, seeds of revolution were sown in the eighteenth-century, and the echoes of the past can be found in the old town neighborhoods.

The allure of New Hampshire has been strong for centuries, and those who seek adventure can find it easily in any corner of the state.

But unless you know where to look, you may miss where to find the real bones of history: in the graveyards. There are gravestones in some of the most unlikely places in New Hampshire, and each one has a story to tell. Some belong to legendary individuals; others to local characters who are legendary in their own right but whose stories have long been forgotten. In many ways, the ghosts of the past reach out to the living from the graveyards, beckoning us to find them and hear their stories.

For some people, graveyards are uncomfortable places, and this sentiment is usually tied to superstitious belief. But what we should really be fearful of is forgetting where we come from. There is much to learn and see among the forgotten stones, if you dare to look.

The ancient iron cemetery gates behind the historic Town Meetinghouse in Greenfield display angels and urns, symbols of the resurrection and everlasting life.

Chapter Two
An Early Landscape of Death
COLONIAL BURYING GROUNDS OF THE SEACOAST

According to a book called the *History of Rye* (1905), the earliest graveyards for the settlers of New Hampshire were family burial plots, but as the book notes, most of these grave sites were soon forgotten and neglected by the living.

Up to a comparatively recent date, graveyards were much more numerous in country towns than they are now. In the early days of the colonies there were private burial grounds on many, if not most, of the larger farms; and even where there was a graveyard connected with the parish church, many of the parishioners, either because they were too far away from the churchyard to be able to reach it conveniently, or from sentimental reasons, preferred to bury their dead on the home farm. Family graveyards, larger than the ordinary farm graveyard, and to which were brought for interment the bodies of deceased members of the family and its near connections from all over its town, and sometimes from other towns, were not infrequent. As families decreased in numbers and importance, or emigrated to other parts of the state or county, or died out altogether, and as farms passed out of the line of former ownership, the family and farm burial grounds would cease to be the objects of anyone's care, and the evidences of neglect soon became apparent in the disappearance of walls or fences, the overthrow of marking stones by the action of frost, and the growth of bushes and trees over the graves. With the establishing of public cemeteries, as distinguished from church burial grounds, many of these private graveyards had the remains of those who had been buried in them removed for re-interment; but hundreds of them still exist, most of them in a sadly neglected condition, many of them forgotten; and not a few of them have been obliterated from record, tradition, or memory, and are now beneath cultivated fields, pastures, or forests.

OLD ODIORNE POINT CEMETERY: RYE

The oldest cemetery in the state of New Hampshire is hidden in the woods alongside the Atlantic Ocean, just behind the nineteenth century farmhouse of the Odiorne family. This first colony at Odiorne's Point in Rye was called the Thompson Settlement. David Thompson was given

Believed to be the oldest cemetery in New Hampshire, the Odiorne burying ground is hidden away in the woods.

consent to build a plantation on the Piscataqua River to fish, grow food and trade with the natives in the name of service to God and liberty.

Nineteenth-century historian Charles Brewster wrote the following remarks about the old cemetery:

> *This first cemetery of the white man in New Hampshire, (it) occupies a space of perhaps one hundred feet by ninety, and is well walled in. The western side is now used as a burial-place for the family, but two thirds of it is filled with perhaps forty graves, indicated by rough head and footstones. Who there rest no one now living knows. But the same care is taken of their quiet beds as if they were of the proprietor's own family. In 1631 Mason sent over about eighty emigrants many of whom died in a few years, and here they were probably buried. Here too, doubtless, rest the remains of several of those whose names stand conspicuous in our early state records.*

In 1899, the National Society of Colonial Dames of America decided it was time to erect a monument on the highest piece of land at Odiorne Point to honor the founders of the state of New Hampshire. The spot was selected so that it could be seen from both the land and the sea. A granite monument was commissioned. Its inscription reads:

Here Landed
The First Band of Englishmen
Pioneers in the Planting of
New Hampshire
Consecrating this Soil to the
Service of God and Liberty

The memorial marker sat at the end of what was known as Columbus Road. In 1955, the marker was moved off the bluff and into the old cemetery to protect it from coastal erosion. It wasn't until 2007 that the marker was put back in its original place on the bluff.

There is a sign near the cemetery's entry gate that reads, "Two hundred and eight-two [*sic*] years of Odiorne ownership led to the use of the family name for Odiorne Point State Park. During World War II, the property was a coastal defense known as Fort Dearborne." The sign refers to the fact that, in 1942, the government took 265 acres of the Odiorne property to build Fort Dearborn. The houses were bulldozed, but the cemetery remained, a silent reminder of those who settled the land. The fort was deactivated in 1948, but the land was never returned to the family. The land had become government-surplus property and was sold to the State of New Hampshire in 1961 for $91,000. The state then turned the area into a public park. The historic cemetery is worth visiting and is one of the area's best-kept secrets.

Pine Grove Cemetery: Hampton

For most people, a visit to Hampton, New Hampshire, conjures up images of beautiful beaches and a vibrant seaside community. There is a cemetery located on Winnacunnet Road that many visitors drive past as they head toward the beach. Originally called the Old Burying Ground, it is now known as Pine Grove Cemetery. The grounds are a bit sandy, and the tall pine trees provide plenty of shade. Not long

Hampton's Pine Grove Cemetery is the final resting place for the early settlers of the town.

ago, the old gate was replaced, and the cemetery landscape is regularly maintained.

The earliest record of the cemetery dates back to January 26, 1654, when the grounds were designated. The grounds were deemed to be five-eighths of an acre and ten rods square. For many years, sheep and calves were allowed to graze in the burial ground, which some people believed was actually good for the cemetery, as it controlled the growth of weeds and helped to keep the grass trim. In 1894, Joseph Dow published a book entitled *History of Hampton*. In the book, he describes the disappearance of gravestones in the cemetery: "As sand shifts with the wind and the tide, so do the gravestones in Pine Grove." A 1680 gravestone for a woman named Susanna Smith who, according to records, was "slaine with thunder," was missing for a number of years. It was rediscovered in 1985 during a survey of the cemetery.

After a heavy storm, another gravestone, one that belonged to Edward Gove, appeared. Gove was a representative of the general court and one of the most famous residents in the town's early history. Gove was caught up in complex political matters involving Governor Edward Cranfield. The governor, who had attempted to raise taxes, had made some enemies after a few short months in the office, and he caused quite a commotion in the courts after he changed a handful of town ordinances to suit his own personal agenda. It wasn't long before the governor changed the way political offices were held, and he even made himself the highest in command when it came to jury selection.

Edward Gove, who was a deputy from Hampton, was upset over the governor's actions, so he decided to fight back. He made it his mission to rally a rebellion against the governor and, one day, rode back and forth from Hampton to Exeter, crying, "Liberty and Reformation!" There were eleven men who had taken part in what is now known as Gove's Rebellion, and all of them were arrested and tried for treason. Gove was sentenced to be tortured and executed; however, Governor Cranfield was worried that Gove might escape imprisonment, so he had him shipped over to England, where he was imprisoned in the Tower of London.

In February 1685, King Charles II died, and his brother James II succeeded him. That fall, Edward Gove was pardoned and sent home to Hampton. In December, two leading citizens of the colony visited the governor's home and severely attacked him. A short time later, the governor left the colony for Barbados, never to return. Edward Gove died in Hampton on May 29, 1691.

The cemetery was used for about 150 years, and today, it is believed that there are still a lot of gravestones hidden beneath the surface of the dirt and sand. One fascinating memorial gravestone in Pine Grove was set in 1909 by the Colonial Dames of America and was a replacement for an earlier gravestone. The text on the stone reads:

> *In memory of Rev. Seaborn Cotton*
> *Born at Sea 1633*
> *Graduated at Harvard College 1651*
> *Ordained 1660 Died 1686*
>
> *Rev. John Cotton Born 1658*
> *Graduated at Harvard College 1678*
> *Ordained 1696 Died 1710*
>
> *Rev. Nathaniel Gookin Born 1687*
> *Graduated at Harvard College 1703*
> *Ordained 1710 Died 1734*
>
> *"Blessed are the dead who die in the LORD"*
> *Erected by the Colonial Dames of New Hampshire 1909*

Seaborn was born on the ship *Griffin* that brought his parents to America. He was the son of John Cotton, a famous Puritan minister of the First Church in Boston, Massachusetts.

There is a curious epitaph on Elizabeth Knight's gravestone:

> *In Memory of Mrs Elizabeth Knight*
> *Wife of Mr Joseph Knight who died Nov 26, 1791*
> *Aged 27 Years*
> *"Yes, she was gentle as the twilight breath*
> *Meekly she bow'd her to the frost of Death."*

Another gravestone describes the watery death of a man named James Lewis:

Here is interred James Lewis of
Barnstable Who Was Drownded
Octr. ye 2nd 1773 on his passage from Kennebeck
to Barnstable in the 21st year of his age

The stone wall that surrounds the cemetery is in better shape than most of the gravestones. Should you decide to stop and take a walk through this shady spot, tread carefully, as those who have long been forgotten are just under your feet. Who knows when and what weather disturbance will cause some stones to reappear in future years after your visit.

POINT OF GRAVES: PORTSMOUTH

Probably one of the most incredible and overlooked cemeteries in the state of New Hampshire would be the Point of Graves. The cemetery is located in the oldest city in New Hampshire and near one of the oldest settlements in the country. Portsmouth was founded in 1623 and was originally called Strawbery Banke, so-named for all of the wild strawberries that lined the shore when the original settlers landed. Located along the Piscataqua River, the city remains vibrant and retains its seventeenth-century charm with a large collection of historic homes. The land for the cemetery was given to the town by Captain John Pickering, and while the cemetery officially dates to 1671, it is thought that burials may have taken place as early as 1650. The last burials took place in the mid- to late nineteenth century, and at that point, the cemetery had become overcrowded and was no longer used.

The cemetery is called the Point of Graves because the land that it encompasses used to be surrounded on both sides by water. In fact, the street the cemetery is on was once called Gravesend Street. Deep-water wharves used to run alongside the cemetery and were primarily used by sailing ships and schooners. In the early twentieth century, the wharves were filled in order to turn the area into a park. This section of Portsmouth was once a very rough part of town and also part of

Left: The seventeenth-century cemetery called Point of Graves offers a large collection of original gravestones from the 1600s.

Below: The highly detailed gravestone for William Button was commissioned by his friends and crewmates.

The grave site for Elizabeth Pierce is rumored to be haunted.

The gravestone for Nathaniel Rogers was signed by the stone carver CL, which stood for Caleb Lamson.

the red-light district in the nineteenth century. The water is a bit farther away from the cemetery today, and there is a bridge that was constructed nearby that goes out to Pierce Island, so the landscape is quite different than what it used to be.

Visitors to the cemetery are greeted by a creaky swing gate and an old iron turnstile. Moving through the turnstile is like passing through a portal in time. It was designed to keep the animals out of the cemetery during the seventeenth century, as they would wander the grounds and root up the fresh burials. Turnstiles are a rarity in New England cemeteries, and it's fascinating to imagine who would have passed through it in the three hundred years that it has been there.

There are about 150 gravestones that remain in the cemetery, the oldest dating back to 1683. Also, there are a handful of purple gravestones in the cemetery that are not native New England designs. The stones would have been shipped over from England and used as ballasts on board ships during the seventeenth and eighteenth centuries. The hand-carved details that are visible on the seventeenth-century stones are captivating. The gravestone for William Button depicts angels, complete with tiny eyelashes, leafy skirts and lips. A few stones have initials carved into them. Most of the signed stones have the initials "C.L." at the top, which stands for Caleb Lamson. The Lamson family was a family of stone carvers from Boston, Massachusetts, and only a fraction of their stones are signed. Three of their signed stones can be found in the Point of Graves.

There are also many great epitaphs inscribed on the stones. For instance, the grave of Joshua Lang Huntress, master-at-arms on the ship the *Ranger*, reads, "He bore a lingering sickness with patience and met the King of terrors with a smile." Huntress died in 1802 at the age of fifty. Death was often personified as The King of Terrors during the seventeenth and eighteenth-centuries. Many believed that death was a physical entity that would come for you when your time was due.

Many of the seventeenth-century gravestones feature winged skulls or skull and crossbones. There are a few striking eighteenth-century stones by a stone carver named John Homer, who was from Boston. He often carved large, life-like designs of the skull and crossbones. This design reflected the beliefs of the time, and it served as a reminder to the living that death could happen at any time.

An Early Landscape of Death

Near a pair of John Homer gravestones is the gravestone for Elizabeth Pierce. According to the inscription, she died of consumption in September 1717 at the age of forty-two. Her stone depicts a winged skull with an hourglass on the top, which illustrates the delicate balance between life and death. A closer look at the hourglass reveals that all of the sand is carved out at the bottom to portray that time has run out. The ghost of Elizabeth is one that many have reported encountering in the cemetery. Some people have reported being tapped on the shoulder by someone that they can't see while walking away from her gravestone. First-time visitors to the cemetery have said that they have been drawn to a particular stone, as if it called to them to take a closer look, and most of the time, that grave was Elizabeth's stone.

Pendulum dowsing is a way of connecting with unseen energies and sometimes spirits to communicate and ask questions. The ghost of Elizabeth is said to be very receptive to pendulum dowsing, and many have suggested that those who are interested in contacting spirits try to contact Elizabeth. According to those who have, her spirit isn't trapped on this earth, and she isn't looking to cross over to "the other side." Time also seems to have no meaning for her. Many believe that she reaches out to those who stop by her grave to pay her respects as they walk away.

Some paranormal groups who have investigated the cemetery state that they have collected EVPs (electronic voice phenomena) around Elizabeth's grave and that Elizabeth herself is quite communicative. Other curious souls claim to have taken unusual photographs around her grave as well. The number of unexplained stories and personal experiences involving Elizabeth's grave increase every year.

The grave of Elizabeth Pierce isn't the only haunted grave in the cemetery; in fact, there is still a mystery from an excavation that was done in the nineteenth century. The cemetery originally had underground tombs that were more ornate than would be expected for such a simple burial ground. One such tomb is the Vaughn tomb, which sits in the far western corner of the cemetery. The marble tablet that marked the tomb had broken in half some years ago, so the Vaughn descendants decided to replace the stone. The ground surrounding the site where the Vaughn grave marker originally sat was flat, and there was no indication of what was under the marker until the digging began. A tomb was uncovered during the first day of excavation, after the old marble tablet had been removed. The tablet was six feet, ten inches in length and three feet wide, and no one is sure how this entrance to the tomb could have been used with the heavy tablet over it.

The entrance to the tomb was four feet high and included an archway that measured two feet, six inches wide. It was thought that perhaps there was a rough wooden frame and door to the tomb at one point as well. The archway above the entrance had broken away over the years, but excavators found several fragments that had survived. A variety of artifacts were discovered inside the vault. Numerous pieces of broken crockery, earthenware, oxidized tinware and even an old ball of India rubber were found in the spaces of the archway. The arched tomb is made out of brick and is eight feet, six inches long and eight feet wide. It measures five feet from the floor to the crown of the arch.

Human remains were discovered near the tomb's entrance, and all of the skulls were intact and facing upward. There were no traces of any of the coffins, except for the iron handles that had rusted away. Amazingly, although the tablet only lists four names, twenty-eight well-defined skulls, leg bones and ribs were removed from the tomb. Dr. Shannon of Portsmouth removed the remains to a neighboring building, where he cleaned and classified the bones. He categorized the remains and found that the tomb housed twenty-one adults, four young adults, two children between the ages of five and eight and one infant. Shannon also noted that some of the adult skulls contained full sets of "exceptional" teeth with no appearance of decay. The doctor then sifted through the pile of remains and skillfully reassembled one of the children's skeletons. It was even written in the reports that some of the local physicians made unsuccessful attempts to obtain some of the skulls for professional purposes. On August 20, 1884, all of the excavated remains were carefully placed in a new casket, covered with a box of pine and replaced in the tomb. The entrance was permanently sealed with solid masonry of stone and cement, and a new monument was placed above the tomb. Today, the original marker is on top of this monument and still displays the splitting crack across it.

The east side of the polished monument bears the following inscriptions:

William Vaughan
Emigrated from England about 1660
Member of the Royal Council for N. H. 1680–1715

Major Commandant Provincial Forces.
Justice of the Court of Common Pleas 1680–1686
Chief Justice of the Superior Court 1708–1715
Died 1719

GEORGE VAUGHAN
Son of Wm. and Margaret Vaughan
Born April 13, 1676
Graduated at Harvard Coll. 1696
Justice of the Court of Common Pleas 1707–1715
Lt. Governor of New Hampshire 1715–1717
Died Dec. 1724

ELIZABETH, *wife of Lt. Gov.* GEORGE VAUGHAN
and daughter of Robert Eliot
Died Dec. 7, 1750. Aged 68

On the south side of the monument, there is an inscription for Lieutenant-Colonel William Vaughan:

In Memoriam

Lt. Col. WILLIAM VAUGHAN
Son of Lt. Gov. George and Elizabeth Vaughan
Born Sept. 12, 1703
Graduated at Harvard Coll. 1722
Projected the Expedition against
Louisburg 1745, and successfully led the
Assaulting Column
Died in London Dec. 1746

People have reported photographing red spirits standing in front of this tomb. In a 2006 documentary called *The Nice Man Cometh*, a local man named Lothar Patten relates his own experience with the red ghosts of the Point of Graves. As Lothar describes, the red ghosts come out of the ground and walk through the cemetery. Lothar's account does not portray any sense of fear; rather, he seems to be familiar with the ghosts.

Local writer and historian Thomas Bailey Aldrich once referred to the graveyard itself as being dead due to its overgrown and abandoned condition. For many years, it was nearly impossible to walk the grounds because of the thick thistle barbs, tall grass and wild strawberries that were wrapped around the stones. Today, the burial ground is well maintained by the city, and there is little to obstruct the views of the intricate and ancient gravestones. A visit to the Point of Graves yields a collection of fascinating ghost stories and remarkable gravestones that connects us with the earliest settlers of the New Hampshire seacoast.

Brackett Massacre Site: Rye

There is a small path just off of Brackett Road in Rye that reveals several rough fieldstone markers. There is a white historic marker that marks this place as the site of the Brackett Massacre. In September 1691, a group of approximately thirty Indians came down the coast from York, Maine, and landed on Sandy Beach. The area settlers were cutting hay and were completely unaware of the threat of danger. The Indians set fire to all of the homes and attacked the settlement. The settlers sent for help, but by the time it arrived, it was too late. Ten dead bodies were found, along with the remains of three people who had burned in the house fires. Seven people were also missing. The footprints of the Indians and their captives were found in the sand. Anthony Brackett, his wife and Francis Rand—three of the village's original settlers—were killed, and the Brackett children were taken prisoner. The Indians dashed the heads of the children who were too young to be held captive against a large rock that once stood on Wallis Road, near what is now Brackett Road. According to local legend, the rock bore the stains of blood for many years. It was removed when the road was improved. Many years later, the Brackett daughter returned from Canada to claim a piece of her father's estate. She had married a Frenchman, and she received the proceeds from the sale of seven acres to satisfy her claim.

It was written that the wife of Francis Rand, who was quite old and blind, had a premonition before the massacre. She claimed to have

Just beyond the sign for the Brackett Massacre site lies the graveyard for those who were killed in 1691.

sensed that Indians were lurking around their neighborhood and felt that she didn't want to be left alone. Mr. Rand seemed unconcerned and went about his business, stating that the closest Indians were at Lake Winnipesaukee. Later that day when Mr. Rand returned home, he discovered his wife had been murdered and scalped by the Indians.

The graveyard is in a shady spot that is surrounded by mature oak and pine trees, and a deep carpet of leaves and pine needles surround the stones. There are no carvings on the rough stones; rather, they stand silently in two rows. People claim to hear screams and shouts echoing in the area when there appears to be no one around. Those who believe in ghosts say the screams belong to those who were massacred. Others believe that the story of the horrifying event is enough to make one believe the area is haunted.

PINE HILL CEMETERY: DOVER

On March 29, 1731, the Pine Hill Burial Ground was established at a town meeting. The town record states: "Voted, That there be one acre & an half of Land Granted for the use of the Town for ever, for a publick Burying-place, To be Laid out by ye select men near ye meeting-house on pine-hill at Cochecha."

At one point, the cemetery was one of the largest in New Hampshire; the grounds covered approximately seventy-five acres and had its own network of roads that stretched seven and a half miles. There are a variety of gravestones in the cemetery, the oldest of which sit near the Central Avenue side. A few toothy-winged skulls can be found on the stones, and there are a number of graves with angels and Victorian sculptures. There

A grinning, toothy skull stands in the Pine Hill Cemetery in Dover.

are many Gothic-styled monuments on a sloping hill toward the center of the cemetery. As the cemetery extends back and across the street, the markers become simpler and less ornate, which these graves are more recent.

One of the most fascinating stories in the cemetery is that of Lucy Lambert Hale. Her gravestone reads, "Lucy Hale Chandler, Wife of Sen. William E Chandler, Jan. 1, 1841, Oct. 15, 1915." Her story is one of romance, intrigue and national tragedy. Lucy was said to be quite an appealing young lady, and many suitors admired her at an early age. Oliver Wendell Holmes Jr., son of the famous poet, met her on vacation in Maine, and after she returned home, he stayed in close correspondence, sending her love letters. She was only seventeen.

Lucy also caught the eye of Robert Todd Lincoln, the oldest son of President Abraham Lincoln. Lucy's father, a prominent senator, had hoped that the two would marry. While their romance was short-lived, they remained good friends throughout the years. In April 1861, at the onset of the Civil War, Lucy and her family moved to Washington, D.C., and once again, Lucy attracted much attention from the community, as demonstrated by a Valentine's Day letter written in 1862:

> *My dear Miss Hale, were it not for the License which a time-honored observance of this day allows, I had not written you this poor note…You resemble in a most remarkable degree a lady, very dear to me, now dead and your close resemblance to her surprised me the first time I saw you. This must be my apology for any apparent rudeness noticeable.*
>
> *To see you has indeed afforded me a melancholy pleasure, if you can conceive of such, and should we never meet nor I see you again—believe me, I shall always associate you in my memory, with her, who was very beautiful, and whose face, like your own I trust, was a faithful index of gentleness and amiability. With a Thousand kind wishes for your future happiness I am, to you, A Stranger.*

The intriguing letter was sent to twenty-one-year-old Lucy from John Wilkes Booth. Booth was a stage actor with a reputation for being a notorious ladies' man. He was handsome and had a magnetic personality and dedicated following of female fans. Based on accounts, the romantic approach that Booth took with Lucy was rather unusual.

The prospect of marrying a senator's daughter certainly held quite a lot of appeal for Booth as well. Lucy was immediately charmed by the charismatic Booth, and not long after they started spending time together, they were secretly engaged.

President Lincoln's second inauguration took place on March 4, 1865, and Lucy had given Booth a ticket to attend. Booth reportedly said, "What an excellent chance I had, if I wished, to kill the President on Inauguration day!" At the time, Booth was engaged in a plot to kidnap President Lincoln and hold him hostage in exchange for the release of Southern prisoners that were held in Union army camps. However, the plan was never carried out, so Booth, a well-known Confederate sympathizer, came up with another idea to assassinate the president.

It wasn't long before the couple began to have disagreements, and Booth's jealousy of Lucy's close friendship with the president's son set him off. Shortly after the inauguration, Booth stayed at the National Hotel in Washington and spent more and more of his time engaged in secret meetings, though it is believed that Lucy knew nothing of his motive.

Lucy's father opposed her relationship with Booth, and near the end of his senatorial term, he approached President Lincoln about a new position. The president appointed Lucy's father as ambassador to Spain, which would help put a distance between the young couple.

On the morning of April 14, 1865, witnesses reported seeing Booth and Lucy in deep conversation in a room at the National Hotel. Lucy spent the rest of the day studying Spanish with Lincoln's son. Meanwhile, Booth learned that the president would be attending a performance at Ford's Theatre that evening, and he put his plan into motion. After having dinner with Lucy and her mother that evening, he lovingly bade his sweetheart goodbye. Almost an hour later, Booth walked into the theater and killed President Lincoln with a single gunshot wound to the head.

Lucy was shocked and saddened by the death of the president, and when she heard a letter was found that connected Booth to the murder, their engagement was over. Immediately after the shooting, Booth fled to Maryland. He was pursued, however, and was eventually found hiding in a barn in Virginia. He was captured and killed, and Lucy's photograph (along with the photos of four other women) was found in his pocket.

Lucy went with her father to Spain. She was courted by many men in the five years she spent abroad, but she was not interested in marriage.

In 1870, Lucy and her family returned to America, but soon after, her father became quite ill, and she took to tending to his needs at their home in Dover until he died in 1873. She was approached by a man named William Chandler some time after her father's death. Chandler had expressed an interest in her some years before her relationship with Booth, and after exchanging a series of passionate love letters, the two were married in 1874.

Chandler was a politician, and he was soon appointed secretary of the navy and United States senator. The couple lived in both Washington and New Hampshire and finally settled in New Hampshire after Chandler finished his service. A statue was placed at the state house in Concord in memory of Lucy's father, and today, it stands with statues of other famous New Hampshire men, including Daniel Webster, President Franklin Pierce and John Stark. Lucy passed away in 1915, and William died two years later in 1917.

Chapter Three

Merrimack Valley and the Capital Area

OLD NORTH CEMETERY: CONCORD

Old North Cemetery is located on North State Street behind restored iron gates and is just down the road from the state capitol. This was Concord's first cemetery and was established in 1730 when the city was known as Penny Cook Township. The cemetery remained in use for 130 years, and in 2008, it was listed on the National Register of Historic Places.

The cemetery is the final resting place for Franklin Pierce, the fourteenth president of the United States and the only president born in New Hampshire. Pierce, known as "Young Hickory of the Granite Hills," was born in 1804 and served as president from 1853 to 1857. He is buried next to his wife, Jane, who died in 1863. Sadly, they both outlived each of their three children. Their first son died just three days after he was born. Their second child, Frank Robert Pierce, died at the age of four in 1843 from typhus, and he is buried with them in the cemetery. Benjamin Pierce, their third child, died in 1853 while the family was traveling on the Boston and Maine Railroad between Andover and Lawrence, Massachusetts. Their train car derailed and fell down an embankment. Eleven-year-old Benjamin was the only casualty.

Jane never recovered from her grief over the loss of all three of her children, and she tried to discourage her husband from running for president. She slipped into a deep depression and contracted tuberculosis.

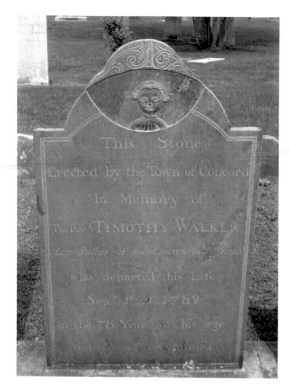

Left: The portrait of Reverend Timothy Walker in Concord is a stylized reflection of typical eighteenth-century attire.

Below: The Old North Cemetery in Concord is the final resting place of Franklin Pierce, the country's fourteenth president.

When Franklin's term was over, he took his wife to the Caribbean and Mediterranean for medical treatment. Despondent and slowly withering away, Jane carried her son's bible and locks of hair from all three of her children until her dying day. Franklin returned to Concord and buried his wife, but his life was never the same afterward. He became reclusive and turned to alcohol in his final years. He died from an inflamed stomach in 1869 at the age of sixty-four. A single granite spire in the Minot Enclosure section of the cemetery marks the Pierces' graves.

There are also graves in the cemetery that refer to the tragic Indian Massacre that took place in August 1746. The town had several garrison houses for protection in case of an Indian attack, and the citizens could barricade themselves inside for safety. Lieutenant Jonathan Bradley arrived in town on August 8, with a band of ten militiamen to help safeguard the town. During Sunday church services the next day, Indians were seen outside, but no attack was made. On Monday, Lieutenant Bradley and seven other men went out to scout for Indians. One man in the group, Daniel Gilman, saw a hawk flying ahead of them, and he ran to shoot it.

The Indians were lying in ambush, waiting for the rest of the party to catch up as a group. Daniel spotted the ambush, and the Indians shot at the men. Lieutenant Bradley cried out in desperation for the men to fight. Daniel ran to the garrison house for assistance. During that time, the Indians killed four men in the group, including Lieutenant Bradley's brother Sam. Some of the men surrendered, but not Bradley. The Indians tomahawked Bradley to death and scalped all the dead. The bodies were brought into town by cart and put on view at Osgood's tavern. The townspeople were shocked and deeply saddened by what they saw. One of the men in the group, Alexander Roberts, escaped from the Indians and was able to tell the tale of what happened.

There is a memorial stone (erected in 1837) in the cemetery that reads: "This monument in memory of Samuel Bradley, Jonathan Bradley, Obadiah Peters, John Brown and John Lufkin who were massacred August 11, 1746, by the Indians."

FOREST HILL CEMETERY: EAST DERRY

Seven towns once made up Nutfield, New Hampshire, including Londonderry, Derry and Windham. Originally settled by sixteen Scotch-Irish families in 1719 that were seeking religious and political freedom, the settlement is rich with culture and history. Just three years after the town was settled, Forest Hill Cemetery was laid out behind the First Settler's Church. The front section of the thirty-five acre cemetery contains the oldest burials and gravestones, and the cemetery is still being used as you head down the lanes towards the back.

A sign at the entrance gate reads:

Forest Hill Cemetery has been the final resting place of Derry's Citizens since 1722. On this hilltop are buried the pioneers of the Nutfield Colony who left their homes in the old world in 1718 to seek freedom in the frontier wilderness of America. Here for eternity rest the veterans of a dozen wars, our first 6 ministers, the town's leaders and thousands of Derry citizens who have together labored to make this town a community.

Lucy Gregg's stone is one of the gravestones located at the cemetery's entrance. Surrounded by a white picket fence, her gravesite holds an honored place in the town's history. Joseph Gregg and Lucy Warner-Gregg were married late in life at the ages of forty and forty-one. They lived in a beautiful Federal-style house built in 1810. On March 6, 1822, Lucy gave birth to little Lucy, which surprised many people in town because they thought that Lucy was too old to have children. Little Lucy was loved by all the townspeople, and because of her kind and generous nature, she was a role model for all of the young people in town.

At the age of twenty-one, Lucy captured the heart of a young man in town, and they were hopelessly in love. Their wedding was set for October 5, 1843. Sadly, a typhus epidemic gripped the town just days before the couple was to be married. Lucy became ill and died the night before her wedding, and her fiancé was devastated. Lucy's family gave the young man the honor of designing her grave marker, and he chose an excerpt from a poem by the British poet Anna Leticia Barbauld. He also decided to build a white picket fence around her grave to protect it. Some

The grave site for Lucy Gregg, who died from typhus the night before her wedding, has quite a story to tell.

legends say that the fence was built to protect her purity. After a long period of mourning, the young man eventually found another woman to marry, and they named their first child Lucy.

The fence was cared for by the townspeople for many years, and in 2010, it was restored by Jim King, a descendant of the Gregg family. The inscription on the gravestone reads:

LUCY
Daughter of
JOSEPH & LUCY
GREGG
died
Oct. 4, 1843
Aged 22 yrs
So fades a summer cloud away
So sinks the gale when storms are o'er

So gently shuts the eye of day
So dies a wave along the shore

The cemetery is filled with every variety of gravestones, all of which were designed in New England. There are several table-stones, primitive stones, tall slates and marble markers. Graves carved with winged skulls, sad faces and upside coffins fill the oldest section. A weathered gravestone from 1747 displays five upside-down coffins.

The gravestone for Dr. Philip Godfrid Kast is one of the most elaborate gravestones in the cemetery. The inscription is as follows:

He was a Gentleman of extensive acquaintance & his benevolence was no less Confine. His hospitality was without Ostentation—In a word he was a benefactor to mankind in his Last Sickness his pain was extream [sic] which he endured with a truly philosophick [sic] Spirit, Without ye Least repining almost beyond example. He left an inconsolable widow & five Small children join'd by the multitude to the loss of a tender husband, an indulgent parent & and valuable friend.
He departed this life Sept 6th 17—.

The stone is about five feet tall and is made of a very dark, fine slate. It also features several intriguing designs associated with the freemasons: a moon and sun with human faces, seven stars, various stone workers' tools, a coffin, a shoe, a book and three candles. Below the designs is the phrase "Virtue and silence." In 1920, the local Masonic lodge took up a collection to reset the stone in a cement frame. It is not known why the year of death is not recorded on the gravestone. The footstone was unearthed in 1993 and placed near the stone.

A tilting sign in front of the earliest graves (which are grouped together behind a metal fence) reads, "First Settler." The inscriptions on the stones are quite fascinating, such as the stone for Charter John Moor. The stone has a map carved on it with an inscription below it that reads:

Born Feb 13, 1692 In a Malt Kiln Glencoe, Scotland
Lived in Antrim County Ireland
Until he was 27 years old

Above: The dramatic gravestone for John Reid is reminiscent of seventeenth-century stones found in England.

Right: The large variety of Masonic symbols on Dr. Philip Godfrid Kast's gravestone tell viewers a little bit more about his level of involvement with the Masons.

Came to Londonderry, NH 1720.
Died about July 1741.
Surveyor, Farmer, Christian.
Erected by his Great, Great, Great, Great Granddaughter Dorothy
Moore, Wife of SD Guess of Whitehall, SC.

Two of the gravestones in the cemetery appear in *Ripley's Believe it or Not* books. The gravestone for Mr. and Mrs. Ewins features an angel, an hourglass and an error: instead of "My Glass is Run," the stone reads, "My Glass is Rum." The other stone belongs to Lizzie James Angell and reads, "I don't know how to die."

Peculiar faces with odd expressions are carved into some of the eighteenth-century gravestones. An expressionless face with a straight horizontal line for a mouth seems to float amongst clouds. A frowning and distraught face can be found on the stone for James Boyce (carved in 1779). Wonderful old iron gates displaying ornate grapevines and musical lyres can also be found. The cemetery is maintained by the Friends of Forest Hill Cemetery, and many of the broken and unreadable stones have been repaired. Should you decide to visit the cemetery, be sure to allow extra time so that you can see all the unusual details the graves have to offer.

Old Bedford Cemetery: Bedford

Hidden just behind the trees along Back River Road is Old Bedford Cemetery, the oldest cemetery in Bedford, New Hampshire. The area was set aside in 1737 as a burial ground. Today, the oldest readable stone is from 1745. The cemetery served as a burial place for the town's first settlers and their families. A walk down a narrow path and up a hill reveals an old hitching post that would have been used by cemetery visitors. The first gravestone near the entrance is surrounded by a low stone wall and is broken. The following inscription is all that is available: "Farewell mother, thou hast left us, And thy loss we deeply feel."

There are many unique gravestones in the cemetery, including the gravestone in the back corner, which reads: "This stone is erected by

The old Bedford Cemetery on Back River Road dates back to 1737.

Lieut. James Moor to the memory of Peter Moor (a Negro servant of William Moor's Elder). He died July 9th 1790 in the 59th year of his age."

A rough, primitive-looking stone with an upside-down coffin reads: "Here lyes the body of Mrs. Mary Patton. She departed this life, October 21st, 1764 aged 81 years. All must obey when death says come and make a bed of earth your home."

There are several gravestones for families who lost several children. One gravestone is for the seven children of John and Sarah Bell, all of whom died between the years 1756 and 1777. Another sad gravestone is for the three children of Major John and Martha Dunlap. Each child died on the day he or she was born, in 1777, 1778 and 1789, respectively.

The Elder children's gravestone is one of the most unusual gravestones in the cemetery. The gravestone depicts four solemn faces, and a matching footstone can be found nearby.

The oldest graves in the cemetery belong to Ann Burns (who died July 1745) and John Patten (1746), who is listed as the father of the Honorable Matthew Patten.

According to the town history book, the cemetery was still being used occasionally in 1851, and it was deemed a place of "solemn resort and profitable meditation." The book also notes, "Here, within the sound of the railroad whistle, the forefathers sleep. Here we stand where tears were shed a hundred years ago for departed friends. Here is still the old stone horse block, where mothers and wives and sisters mounted, having followed in procession some loved one to the grave."

The cemetery still retains an air of peacefulness concealed behind the trees of Bedford.

VALLEY CEMETERY: MANCHESTER

Manchester has long been a city of industry along the Merrimack River and was the home to the Amoskeag Manufacturing Company in the nineteenth and early twentieth centuries. In 1840, the company donated approximately twenty acres to the city to be used as a cemetery. The area, once considered the edge of town, is now bordered by Auburn Pine Valley and Willow Streets. According to the conditions of the deed written in 1840, the land was to be "used for no other purpose than for burying." Modeled after the garden-style Mount Auburn Cemetery in Cambridge, Massachusetts, the cemetery was not only a place to bury the dead but was also an arboretum and oasis, inviting visitors to walk its paths and enjoy the shade of the hundreds of beautiful, shady trees. Couples would take Sunday sojourns through the cemetery, enjoy carriage rides or have picnics. Old postcards of the cemetery depict a lovely gazebo surrounded by walking paths.

In the 1850s, Manchester was hit by a cholera epidemic, and every night, another person was buried in a mass grave in the cemetery. The mass grave is in the northeast corner of the cemetery; however, there are very few headstones that record the names of those who are buried there.

Right: The chapel in Valley Cemetery is rumored to be haunted by phantom voices.

Below: Toppled gravestones in Valley Cemetery have had to be repaired continuously over the years.

In the northwest corner of the cemetery is a pauper's area, and most of the graves there are also unmarked.

As the population of Manchester grew along with the prosperity of the mill, the cemetery began to fill quickly, and almost all of the burial plots in the cemetery were sold by 1859. For many years during the nineteenth century, Manchester residents would visit the cemetery on Decoration Day (which is now observed as Memorial Day) and pay their respects to Civil War veterans. Local schoolchildren decorated veteran graves with wreaths and evergreens while the city band played patriotic music.

In 1888, the city tomb was constructed in the hillside of Valley Cemetery and served as a place to store the deceased during the winter months. The tomb cost $4,000. In recent years, the accumulation of brush and overgrowth was finally cleared away to once again reveal the large doors of the tomb. In May 1888, a boiler explosion at a nearby factory rocked the neighborhood. Several people were killed, and the debris from the blast was heaved into the cemetery, breaking many gravestones.

A beautiful English Gothic chapel featuring praying angels over the entrance door was built in the cemetery in 1932. Sadly, the chapel hasn't been used for years; the stained glass windows have been broken out and boarded up. Visitors to the cemetery claim to hear disembodied voices and the cries of a woman emanating from the within.

One of the most impressive mausoleums in the cemetery is that of Governor Smythe, who served from 1865 to 1867. The mausoleum sits on the edge of a high bluff and was designed to resemble a Greek temple. The outer walls are marred by graffiti, but the mausoleum itself remains in relatively good condition. It is rumored that the soft sobs of a woman who was murdered near the mausoleum can be heard by passersby.

Inside Valley Cemetery is a smaller cemetery that contains the remains of early settlers that were disinterred from Christian Brook Cemetery when the railroad pass was built in the nineteenth century. A slate headstone in the southwestern corner of Valley Cemetery marks the spot where the remains of Archibald Stark now lie. The headstone reads, "Here Lyes the Body of Mr. Archibald Stark, He departed this life June 20th 1758, Aged 61 years." Archibald was the brother of Revolutionary War hero General John Stark, who is credited for saying "Live Free or Die"— the official motto for New Hampshire. Recreational visitors no longer visit the cemetery as they once did. The waters of a sparkling natural brook that once meandered through the grounds now mix with odorous city sewage and are directed through an underground culvert to the Merrimack River. Family mausoleums and tombs have been vandalized and spray painted with graffiti that is difficult and costly to remove. The once majestic and towering trees slowly decayed and were removed some years ago as they posed a risk to the monuments and statues. Today, an organization known as the Friends of the Valley Cemetery is working to raise funds in order to bring respect and grandeur back to the cemetery.

Chapter Four

White Mountains and the Great North Woods

WILLOW CEMETERY: FRANCONIA

Willow Cemetery is just off the road that leads from Franconia to Easton. The ornate, arched sign is bordered by tall pines, and there's a slight slope up a hill into the clearing where rows of white marble gravestones dating to the nineteenth century can be found. George Maxwell's gravestone sticks out from the others; it sits in its own row at the very front in the right corner of the cemetery. According to the inscription, George was sixty-four years old when he died on December 8, 1866. But a walk behind the stone reveals a chilling inscription: "Killed by Samuel Mills." The terrifying events that unfolded on the night of December 8 soon became part of the public record.

Samuel was a local laborer who worked at the Dodge Gold Mine. It was hard work, and he received very little pay. He had recently stolen a gold watch from a fellow co-worker, which had aroused some suspicion about his character. Word around town was that a local man, George Maxwell, had recently sold some real estate and that he might have the cash from the sale on his property. So, on a dreadful stormy night, Samuel made the long walk to George's farmhouse. Twenty-four-year-old Samuel had plenty of time to form a plan during his walk, and he was quite ready for anything when he reached his destination.

Above: The Willow Cemetery in Franconia features an ornate entrance gate.

Left: The back of George Maxwell's gravestone states that he was killed by Samuel Mills.

When George opened the door, he knew immediately that something was wrong. According to records, the men fought each other violently. The end came when Samuel picked up an axe and embedded it into George's neck. Samuel's search for the money turned up nothing, so he took George's horse and wagon. The horse's attitude in the foul weather, however, forced Samuel to abandon the wagon in the village, and he disappeared into the night. Eventually, Samuel made it to Canada and finally out to the American West.

Meanwhile, in Franconia, George's body was discovered, and there was enough evidence to suspect Samuel of the crime. Sketches and wanted notices were drawn up and distributed throughout the region. Eventually, Samuel was detained for another crime in Illinois, where it was discovered that he was wanted in New Hampshire. He was returned to Haverhill, New Hampshire, to await his fate. The jury found him guilty, and he was sentenced to hang on May 6, 1868. Three thousand people showed up to witness the hanging. On the wall in his prison cell, Samuel scrawled, "Samma Mills, murder going to be hung today of May—good man but no man don't know it."

Some people believe George Maxwell was buried in his own row because his spirit can't rest beyond the grave. Others believe that the townspeople were so distraught over what happened that they chose a special place for him at the front of the cemetery.

Henry Houghton's grave can also be found in the cemetery. Henry had moved from Newfane, Vermont, to work at the Upper Iron Works, which was located along the Gale River in the village. Not long after he moved, Houghton had a strange dream that foretold his death. Houghton reportedly dreamt that he accidentally injured the upper part of his leg while working with an adz (a sharp cutting tool used for cutting rough wood) and that he would die from the injury within a certain number of days. He also said that he would be buried in a place that he had never seen.

Houghton was so convinced that the dream would come true that he told his wife about it the following morning. A few days later, Houghton came home from work and told her that he had seen the place where he was going to be buried. Within a week, he cut his leg with an adz while working on a dam at the ironworks. The moment he arrived home, he told his wife, "I am a dead man." Houghton died the day he had predicted, on November 1, 1827. His grave can be found toward the back of the cemetery. The marble stone cracked in half some years ago, but it is still readable.

The Grave of the White Mountain Hermit, English Jack: Twin Mountain

The story of John (Jack) Vials, known by the locals as English Jack, reads like a fantastical movie script. Author James E. Mitchell chronicled the early days of English Jack's life back in 1891. Jack became an orphan in the 1830s, at the age of twelve. He was taken in as a cabin boy and became an able seaman in just a few short years. The Simmonds family treated Jack like family, and he came to care for them deeply.

While on a voyage to the Indian Ocean with Mr. Simmonds, the ship ran into a hurricane and was wrecked. Only thirteen of the forty-two men on board managed to make their way onto a barren island. They were stranded on the island for nineteen months with nothing to eat but mussels, crabs, limpets and snakes when they could catch them. Jack was finally rescued by an American ship. Unfortunately, Captain Simmonds did not survive. When Jack returned to England, he learned that Mrs. Simmonds had died and that her daughter, Mary, had been sent to a workhouse. Jack eventually found Mary, and soon, their close friendship turned into love, and they decided to marry. Jack decided to take on one more seafaring voyage so that they would have enough money to start their lives. Mary enrolled in boarding school and Jack sailed off, hoping to return to a new future with his wife-to-be. Sadly, when Jack returned from his venture, he found that Mary had died, and once again, he was all alone.

Jack sank into a depression. Nearly a year after Mary's death, he joined the Royal Navy, hoping that a "kind death" would take him. But Jack's ventures only brought him new sights and experiences. Around 1870, word began to spread that a railroad connecting Portland, Maine, to areas in upstate Vermont and New York was being built. The plans for the railroad included building a new pass at Crawford Notch in the

White Mountains. Jack signed on as a worker, and when the railroad was completed in 1875, he decided to stay in the White Mountains. He began collecting bits of scrap wood that he found, along with iron sheeting and a couple of doors, and he used these to construct a rambling dwelling that he called "his ship." Jack lived in his ship for almost thirty-five years, but he spent his winters with two families in the Twin Mountains. But as soon as winter was over, he went right back to his ship in Crawford Notch.

Just north of Jack's ship was the beautiful Crawford House, which has served as a travel destination for nearly one hundred years. The guests of the Crawford House were also guests of Jack's ship, and they could often be seen taking the woodland trail from the inn to "The House that Jack Built," as the sign at the trailhead said. Various trees along the trail had red ribbon tied around them and featured little faces that had been carved into their knots. Jack would regale his visitors with stories of his adventures and life in the Notch. Jack even sold a little book of verse about his life before 1870 and lived off the money he made from the sales.

Here is an excerpt from one is his poems:

> *When they finished their railroad I figgered I'd steer*
> *Fer permanent moorin's in the mountains round here.*
> *So I built this 'ere cabin—such as she are*
> *And I'll stick to the ship 'till I drift cross the bar.*

He also sold other memorabilia, such as postcards that pictured him standing in front of his ship. According to accounts, he would eat live frogs and snakes in front of his guests for twenty-five cents. In addition, Jack kept a brown bear and was the first official bear trainer in New Hampshire. He even kept a trout pool near his ship and would throw in scraps of bread to feed them.

On April 24, 1912, "kind death" finally paid English Jack a visit. His obituary was printed in the *New York Times*:

> *English Jack known to all visitors of the White Mountains as the*
> *Crawford Notch Hermit is dead. He was said to be 90 years old,*

and lived in an old shanty, which he called his "ship" and where he made a famous home brewed beer that refreshed many a pilgrim on a mountain tramp.

The locals paid to have a gravestone set for Jack in Straw Road Cemetery in Twin Mountain and even created a fund to take care of it. "The Hermit of Crawford Notch" is written across the top of the stone.

WILLEY FAMILY GRAVEYARD: NORTH CONWAY

At first glance, the Stonehurst Manor, located on Route 16 in North Conway, seems an unlikely place to find a family graveyard. But hidden behind a stone wall, underneath the tall pine trees, lies the Willey family plot. The gravestone marker tells the terrifying tale of what happened on the night of August 28, 1826. In the fall of 1825, Samuel Willey Jr., his wife, five children and two hired men moved from Bartlett into the heart of Crawford Notch, which is about ten miles away from Mount Washington. In June 1826, a severe storm cut a path of destruction through the mountains. A slide came off of the mountain behind the Willeys' house, pushing trees, boulders and earth across the nearby road

After the family's frightening experience, Samuel decided to build a shelter just south of the house in case there was another slide. That August, another severe storm hit the area. The Saco River rose twenty feet and flooded the Notch and the rest of the valley as far as Conway. Two days after the storm, anxious friends and family of the Willeys' came to their home to see how the family had fared. When they arrived, there was no sign of the Willey family. However, the group did see that there was a slide off the mountain. Apparently, the slide came down the mountain, hit a rocky ledge and then split, passing both sides of the house. The house remained intact. Inside, the beds were still made, and a bible lay on the table.

No one knows exactly what happened during the slide, but it appeared that the family left the house in order to seek shelter from the rising flood, and in doing so, they ran directly into the path of the landslide. The bodies of Mr. and Mrs. Willey, two of their children and both of their hired men were uncovered in the debris. The other three children were never found. The bodies were buried near the house, but in later years, they were removed and placed in the family graveyard in North Conway.

An urn and two willow trees are engraved in the marble gravestone. The inscription reads:

To the memory of the family which was at once destroyed by a slide from the White Mountains on the night of 28 August, 1826.

Samuel Willey Ae   38
Polly L. Willey   35
Eliza A. Willey   12
Jeremiah L. Willey   11
Martha G. Willey   10
Elbridge G. Willey   7
Sally Willey   3

The Grave of Nancy Barton: Hart's Location

For many years, a sign hung on a tree along a walking trail in Hart's Location that read, "Nancy ———, of Jefferson, NH Perished here in 1778. Following the wild path of the Notch for thirty miles, in a vain attempt to overtake her faithless lover, she perished in a snowstorm by this stream and is buried here. Nancy was the second woman to go through the Notch pass."

According to the story, a young lady named Nancy Barton was working as a maid for Colonel Joseph Whipple when she met a young man named Jim, who was also employed by the Colonel. She fell deeply in love with Jim, and the two made plans to marry. Nancy had managed to save a small sum of money over the years, and she told her beau about it. One day, the colonel asked the young man to ride to Portsmouth with him, and Jim agreed, taking Nancy's money with him. While he was away, Nancy overheard two men talking about the man she was to marry and learned that he was actually on his way to Portsmouth to marry a widow there.

The gravestone of Nancy Barton was never placed over her grave; rather, it stands in the living room of the Notchland Inn.

Upset, Nancy ran after the colonel and Jim, hoping to catch up to them. By the time Nancy reached the Notch wilderness, snow had begun to fall. When Nancy reached the brook, she found signs that the men had camped there. Tired from her difficult trek into the woods, she sat down beside the dying fire they had left. Soon, Nancy was covered in snow, and she lay down on the ground. Her body was found the next day, and she was buried in that same spot, and the grave was marked with stones.

The brook became known as Nancy Brook, and the mountain is called Nancy's Mountain. There is a tombstone in the front parlor at the nearby Notchland Inn. Inscribed on the stone are the words "1778 Died in a snowstorm in pursuit of her faithless lover." The slate gravestone was never placed on her grave, and some people believe that her restless spirit wanders from her burial site along the Nancy Brook Trail to the inn where her gravestone is.

Colebrook Village Cemetery: Colebrook

The town of Colebrook, located in the Great North Woods area of Coos County, was incorporated in 1796. The town cemetery is located on Route 3, which is also known as the Daniel Webster Highway. The cemetery is simple and spacious. Most of the gravestones are from the nineteenth and twentieth centuries. Many of the marble stones are in excellent shape and are easy to read. There is one particularly curious stone in the cemetery that reads:

In Memory of George E. Hodge
Who was killed on this spot by a
load of gravel passing over
His body, June 13, 1884
Æ 31 ys. 9 mos.

Located in Coos County, Colebrook Cemetery features a wide variety of nineteenth-century gravestones.

It's peculiar to think that George may have died on the grounds of the cemetery. The marker, however, originally stood off the side of Route 26. When the road was widened, the marker was removed to a storage shed and was eventually placed in the town cemetery. Ironically, George's actual gravestone also sits in the cemetery, as he was buried there after he was killed.

The Grave of Chief Metallak: Stewartstown

A historic sign on the side of the road in Stewartstown, New Hampshire, reads:

> *Metallak, hunter, trapper, fisherman, and guide, well and favorably known by the region's early settlers as "The Lone Indian of the Magalloway" was the last survivor of a band of Abnaki* [sic] *inhabiting the Upper Androscoggin. Blinded by accidents, Metallak died a town charge in 1847 at the reputed age of 120. He is buried in the North Hill Cemetery on the road to the east.*

Much has been written about Metallak, and most of these writings are based on stories that have been passed down over the years. By all accounts, he was a colorful man with a lot of character who left quite an impression on those he met during his lifetime. According to records, he built his lodge near the Androscoggin River, on land that was once occupied by the Coo-ash-aukes, the tribe his ancestors belonged to. There are also stories that Metallak rode a moose and lived through many wild adventures.

Metallak married twice and had two children. He was said to be deeply in love with his second wife. One day while he was making a pair of moccasins, the needle slipped out of his raised hand and he inadvertently blinded himself in one eye. Years passed, and Metallak's beloved wife became ill and died. Heartbroken, he placed her body in a canoe, along with some of her precious belongings, and traveled along the rivers to Lake Umbagog. There, on an island that now bears Metallak's name, he buried his wife (near what is now Moll's Rock), and he stayed by her grave for three days. He eventually built a hut and lived on the island for a short while. Two hunters found the old chief in the woods some years later. The old man had apparently fallen, blinded himself in his other eye and was suffering from starvation. The men decided to feed and take care of him, and they brought him to Stewartstown. Metallak became a public charge of Coos County, where he spent his final years. He died on the floor in the home of a virtual stranger (he refused to sleep in a bed) that was on land his people once called their own. Some records say that the old chief lived to be 120 years old; others say that he passed away at 102.

The inscription on Metallak's grave, located in North Hill Cemetery in Stewartstown, reads:

> *Metallak the Lone Chief of the Magalloway*
> *Died about 1850*
> *Last of the Coashaukes*
> *Erected 1915 by John H. Emerson*

Tokens of remembrance left by visitors include stones, feathers and walking sticks. His legacy remains one of the most captivating stories of New England's North Country.

Russell-Colbath Cemetery (Albany Cemetery): Passaconaway

A small cemetery along Kancamangus Highway serves as the final resting place for Ruth Colbath, a woman whose devotion to her husband lasted until her death. Ruth's father had purchased five one-hundred-acre lots in the wilderness town of Passaconaway, and the family lived off of the land. When he died in 1877, much of the land was taken to pay off the mortgage and taxes. Ruth, her mother Eliza and her husband Thomas Alden Colbath took up residence in the old homestead and continued to work what little farmland they had left.

One night, in 1891, Thomas told Ruth that he was going out and would be "back in a little while." That night, Ruth set a lit lantern by the

The cemetery gates at the Russell Colbath Historic Site display heavenly harps and arrows pointing to heaven.

window and awaited her husband's return. The days passed and turned into weeks, but there was no sight of Ruth's husband. Nevertheless, she continued to keep a light by the window. In 1905, Ruth's mother passed away, leaving her alone on the farm.

For thirty-nine years, Ruth kept a lit lantern by the window. Finally, in 1930, Ruth passed away at the age of eighty. Three years later, Thomas finally returned to Passaconaway to claim the house and farm. He, however, was too late: the property had already been divided among Ruth's cousins.

Thomas never gave an explanation for his forty-two-year absence. He had all sorts of stories about the adventures he had over the years, none of which checked out. Eventually, Thomas left town, and no one was quite sure where he ended up. Ruth Priscilla Colbath was buried in the village cemetery, along with the rest of her family.

There are at least sixty people who are buried in the cemetery, and Ruth has one of the largest markers on the grounds. The property is now a designated historic site, which is operated by the National Forest Service. It is said that Ruth's spirit cannot rest because her husband never came home, and some have reported seeing her spirit walking from the cemetery toward her house. There are even stories that a phantom light sometimes shines through the front window of the house when there is no one around. Could it be the spirit of Ruth still holding her silent vigil from beyond the grave?

Chapter Five
Monadnock Valley

Old Burying Ground: Jaffrey

The town of Jaffrey was originally named for George Jaffrey, a Masonic proprietor who was from Portsmouth, New Hampshire. Oddly enough, George never actually set foot on the wilderness land that he had invested in. The town was settled around 1758 and was finally incorporated in 1773. Jaffrey retains much of its rural village charm today.

In the summer of 1770, John Grout, who many believed to be one of the first settlers of Jaffrey, died. As the town had not yet established a burial ground, his body was laid to rest in what would eventually become the common area. No marker was placed on his grave, and five years later, a town meetinghouse was built directly over it. Some people believed it fitting that his dust was under the meetinghouse since Grout was one of Jaffrey's first settlers. In 1784, the townspeople decided to establish a "burreing yard" next to the meetinghouse. However, the lot was quickly filled, and residents were already searching for other spots in which to bury their dead before the second generation of residents had completely passed away.

Today, the meetinghouse remains in beautiful condition, and so is the long stable house behind it that leads to the burial ground. There are many long rows of slate stones, and more moss-covered stones can be found at the edge of the hill, scattered underneath the trees.

Left: The old meetinghouse in Jaffrey stands at the entrance to the burial grounds.

Below: Dorothy Caldwell's gravestone, which was carved by her husband, depicts the portrait of his wife.

The rocky ledges of Mount Monadnock tower in the background, just beyond the valley.

In 1778, a Saxon was selected to dig the graves in the burial ground. He was described as "a mighty man, that 'Saxon,' and never ceased his labors until he had gathered the last of the stubborn old pioneers into his narrow field." The gravestones that stand over some of those old pioneers tell fascinating stories. The inscription on the grave of Moses Stickne states that he was the "first child who trod the wilds of Jaffrey."

Two gravestones that are engraved with willows and urns and standing side by side allude to the dark chapters of slavery in New England:

Sacred to the memory of
AMOS FORTUNE
Who was born free in Africa,
a Slave in America.
He purchased his liberty,
Professed Christianity,
Lived reputably,
died hopefully,
Nov. 17, 1801, a. 91

Sacred to the memory of
VIOLATE
by sale the Slave of Amos Fortune,
by Marriage his wife,
by her fidelity, his friend and solace.
She died his widow, Sept. 13, 1802, a. 72

A young African man was brought over as part of the cargo of a slave ship that arrived in Boston Harbor in 1725. He was purchased by a weaver, who taught him how to read and write. The young man was given the name of Amos, and because things seemed to have a way of going well for him, he was called Mr. Fortunus. Eventually, he was simply called Amos Fortune.

He changed masters over the years, learned several trades and, at the age of sixty, was finally able to purchase freedom. He used the profits made from tanning business to purchase his wife Violate's freedom, as well as her eight-year-old child Celyndia. The family then took all of their possessions, left Boston and moved to Jaffrey. Within a year, Amos was able to purchase his own land, and he built a house and barn near a scenic brook. Amos and his family were quite respected and welcomed by Jaffrey's townspeople. He attended church regularly and was quite involved with the community. At the age of ninety-one, he instructed Deacon Spofford, who witnessed Amos's will, to purchase a silver communion service and leave $243 to the local school. For himself, Amos only requested that he and Violate receive "handsome" gravestones in the churchyard. In 1946, an organization called the Amos Fortune Forum was established. The Forum's mission was to organize events throughout the year that featured guest speakers and topics of public interest and importance for those who live in and visit the Monadnock region.

Probably one of the most striking graves in the burial ground is hidden in the western corner under the pine trees. Dorothy Caldwell's grave displays a three-dimensional face and reads, "Wife of Viggo Brandt-Erichsen and infant daughter." The years 1882 and 1926 are also written on the gravestone. Viggo was born in Denmark and was quite an accomplished painter and sculptor, having even worked alongside Pablo Picasso. In 1924, while Viggo was in Paris, he met a beautiful American woman named Dorothy Caldwell. The two fell in love and were married. However, their first child died shortly after it was born. Not long after, Dorothy became gravely ill, and Viggo promised to bury her ashes in the shadow of Mount Monadnock in Jaffrey, New Hampshire. After Dorothy's death, Viggo took both his wife's and his infant child's ashes and set sail for Jaffrey. He moved into a hotel near the town and immediately began work on sculpting a grave marker for his family. The sculpture was completed in two years and not only bears Dorothy's face but also features detailed religious imagery and angels. The sculpture also features scrolled iron bars.

Some years later, Viggo married a woman named Joan Crowley, who ended up dying of cancer. He built a gorgeous monument in Jaffrey for her, complete with forest animals and a reflecting pool. Unfortunately, the memorial was vandalized, and the few pieces that were salvaged were removed. Viggo lived in Jaffrey for twenty-three years and was a well-liked member of the community. He earned his American citizenship and eventually left the town to spend his final years in California. The unusual grave marker dedicated to Viggo's first wife continues to draw visitors today.

The burial ground is also the final resting place for author Willa Cather, who was a regular visitor to Jaffrey. She was a novelist whose work includes novels about frontier life on the plains. She would often write in a tent that was set up in a field with a view of Mount Monadnock. The gravestone of this Pulitzer Prize–winning author is inscribed with a quote from her novel *My Antonia*: "That is happiness to be dissolved into something complete and great."

PHILIPS-HEIL CEMETERY: JAFFREY

The Philips-Heil Cemetery is a breathtaking burial ground located in the southwestern section of Jaffrey, not far from Gap Mountain. The families who lived near this cemetery were slightly removed from the meetinghouse in the center of town, and they formed a close-knit farming community.

The cemetery was established in 1797 by Lieutenant Governor Samuel Philips. His son, Samuel Philips Jr., was the founder of Philips Academy (1778), located in Andover, Massachusetts. Philips also operated a gunpowder mill that provided General George Washington's troops with ammunition during the Revolutionary War. The conditions of the burial ground were laid out as follows: "It should be fenced with a good stone wall…a tract of ninety-five square rods for a burial yard."

The road that leads to the cemetery would be very easily missed were it not for the white sign hanging high from a weathered piece of granite in front of an ancient maple tree. The hilly, grass-covered road doesn't seem to lead anywhere, except toward the deep woods. Surprisingly, the cemetery appears once you crest the last grassy hill and follow the curve. The grounds are completely carpeted in thick moss, and the edges of the cemetery disappear into the forest. Tall trees are home to a variety of birds that dart in and out overhead. The sounds of hawks and crows fill the air, and if you're lucky, you may come across turkey feathers as you walk the grounds.

The large stone chair in the Ross family plot is a place for the spirits of the past to rest.

The gravestones reflect sentiments of sorrow and loss that are sustained and soothed by an unfaltering trust in a better hereafter. Their epitaphs tell the living the lessons the dead had learned in their short life, such as the one below:

> *In memory of HARRIET,*
> *DAUGHTER OF John & Sally Worcester,*
> *who died Jan. 9, 1832. AE. 9 years.*
> *Without a tear without a sigh,*
> *This happy youth alas did die;*
> *Four infant babes beside her rest*
> *While God is pleas'd to call them blessed.*

A double gravestone for the two children of Moses Worcester reads:

'Tis God that lifts our comforts high,
Or sinks them in the grave;
He gives and blessed be His name,
He takes but what he gave.

A gravestone for young David Comstock, who was just eight years old when he died on October 19, 1849, reads:

As you survey this sacred spot,
And think how short on earth my lot,
Improve your time, and now prepare.
That you, the joys of Heaven may share.

And finally, ponder this simple inscription for Roancy Dutton, wife of Jonathan Jewett Comstock, who died May 1, 1883, at the age of seventy-nine: "She hath done what she could."

The life-size granite chair located at the back of the cemetery is the reason why this spot is so legendary. The name on the chair reads, "J. Ross, 1871," and it is part of the Ross family burial plot. The gravestones for the Elder Jonas Ross, who died in 1861, and his wife Nancy, who died in 1876, are accompanied by the graves of their four children, who all died before their time. Two baby boys, both of whom were named Jonas, didn't live long enough to see their first birthday. Their daughter, Persis, died at the age of twenty-one, and their son Martin died at the age of eighteen. Each gravestone features a carved circle that is inscribed with beautiful imagery. Elder Jonas's stone features a hand pointing to the sky and bears the inscription "God is love."

The Ross family lived in the area for three generations, and the stone chair is a fascinating piece that links the past with the future. A spiritual-minded descendant of the Ross family who believed that the souls of the deceased return to the spot of their former existence had the chair placed next to the graves so that their spirits could sit facing the sunset and reflect on their existence on earth. And because the cemetery is so quiet (except for the sounds of nature), one can easily commune with the unseen energies that exist in this fascinating cemetery.

Chapter Six
Bone Chilling Tales

AN UNFORGETTABLE NIGHT: SUNAPEE

Sunapee, New Hampshire, is home to the many-peaked Mount Sunapee and the beautiful Lake Sunapee. The name Sunapee comes from an Algonquian Indian word that means "lake of the wild goose," and indeed, the lake is shaped like a goose. Although not quite the vacation spot it was years ago, Sunapee still draws plenty of visitors to its crystal blue lake every year.

The Eighteenth Amendment prohibited the sale and distribution of alcohol in the United States. During Prohibition, bootlegging became a secret pastime for many thirsty men, but not all bootleggers were professional. Take the story of a thirsty Sunapee man named "Jeff" (his real name is not known). Jeff took it upon himself to not only quench his own thirst but also make a few bucks while doing it. A lot of bootlegging took place under the shadow of the night. Trucks were camouflaged, and cases were secretly tossed from trains in designated spots. Once the alcohol was collected, it would be brought into private homes to be "cut" for resale. (Cutting alcohol is the process of watering it down to make it go further, which maximized bootleggers' profits.)

Jeff was part of a bootlegging ring that sold Canadian whisky, and he developed a secret hiding place no one would have suspected—the local cemetery. It was a perfect spot where Jeff could bury the booze and go back in the middle of the night to dig it up. The dead didn't seem to mind. However, on one particular night visit to the cemetery, Jeff became quite thirsty and decided to do a little quality control on the cases of Canadian whisky. After all, he had to make sure that he had the full twelve imperial quarts he had purchased, so he figured he might as well taste test the booze too. Jeff sampled case after case. There was no chance that he would be thirsty on the way back home.

By the time Jeff lugged the fourth case of whisky out of the cemetery, he was feeling no pain. In fact, his limbs were warmed by the booze. The fifth case, however, felt heavier than the previous ones. When he finally returned to his front yard, he set down his load and passed out on the lawn.

A passing neighbor woke up Jeff just after dawn the next day, and the bootlegger discovered that he had brought home a gravestone from the cemetery instead of a case of alcohol. Jeff got up and quickly dragged the slab back to the cemetery. Word of the incident soon spread throughout the town, and many wondered which crooked gravestone marked the spot where the amateur bootlegger kept his stash.

A Bewitching Mystery: New Hampton

Gravestones dot the hilly terrain of Village Cemetery in the town of New Hampton. The cemetery is probably one of the best places to see the sunset in the little town, and it's also one of the best places to find a witch's grave. Peaceful, small towns often have some of the most dramatic tales.

Esther Prescott Hyde's house stood in what was described as a lonely spot in town. According to accounts, Esther was kind and gentle with the town children, and they loved her. Regular visits with the younger generation were encouraged and appreciated by both parties. But a simple misunderstanding changed everything.

A few suspicious people in town gossiped about Esther because she never spoke about her family or her past. Rumors began to spread that she was a witch, and some of the adults refused to speak to her. Some even referred to her as Granny Hicks. One day, she went to a neighbor's house in the village to borrow some yarn for a stocking that she was knitting, and she was refused admittance. The next morning, a woodchuck was seen on the doorstep of the same house, and that night, the infant child who lived in the house became ill and died. Many suspected that Esther had bewitched the child, and the townspeople immediately became fearful for their lives as well as their livestock.

A few nights after the child's death, five local boys who had spent the evening drinking rum decided to go to Esther's home. Donning masks, the boys took their axes, made their way to the woman's home and set it on fire. Esther pleaded with them, but the house burned to the ground. Finally, she climbed on top of a tree stump, pointed her finger at each of the boys, called their name and detailed how they would die. She left town not long afterward.

Dr. A.J. Gordon, a famous preacher from Boston, heard about Esther's curse, and he followed the fate of the boys. All five boys died just as the woman predicted. Gordon felt that there were eternal laws of retribution that were as certain as the order of the heavens. The doctor believed that Esther was a poor soul who had been wrongly accused of sorcery and who may have received super-human abilities due to her plight. Her words, the doctor declared, were wiser than she ever knew.

Esther returned to New Hampton a few years later. She died on April 14, 1817 and was buried in Village Cemetery, on a hill that overlooks the mountainside. No birth date is listed on her gravestone. Instead, the stone simply states that she was the wife of J.H., which adds more to the mystery of her life. Should you visit her grave, bring some flowers: Esther might appreciate your thoughtfulness.

FAXON HILL ROAD CEMETERY (WASHINGTON CENTER CEMETERY): WASHINGTON

Faxon Hill Road Cemetery in Washington, New Hampshire, has much to offer curiosity seekers. The first settlers arrived in the area in 1768, and the settlement was simply known as Number 8. On December 13, 1776, the town was incorporated as Washington, in honor of George Washington. At one point, there were several secret societies in town. One group would hold secret meetings in a hotel that would eventually become known as the Lovell House. Today, Washington is a quaint, country town with a population of less than one thousand. The gravestones in the cemetery provide an interesting glimpse into the area's history.

There are three interesting markers in the cemetery that aren't actually gravestones; rather, they are Gothic cast-iron markers that date between the 1840s and 1850s. They are all completely identical, except for the differences between lettering and size. The marker for Caroline Chipman, who died in 1850 at the age of five, has a plate on its back that reads, "Greenleaf & Newman, Hillsboro Br. N.H." There are approximately only fifteen of these types of markers in the Hillsborough, New Hampshire region, which makes them quite unique. Some indications on these markers suggest that they may have been painted white to resemble

Gothic cast-iron grave markers, such as the one pictured here, are a rarity in New Hampshire.

white marble gravestones, but today, most of these stones are covered in patina.

Cathedral-style Gothic arches engraved into the markers include columns and spires, but the cast is less than an inch thick. A double-sided mold would have been used to create the marker. This type of ironwork was called "flask casting" and required the use of wooden box frames and sand. To cast these markers, iron would be poured through a "gate" (a large frame-like structure) and then left to cool and form. Because these iron markers are quite rare, it is likely this gravestone style was not widely accepted among those in the trade.

Many of the slate markers in the cemetery are quite tall, some measuring as much as four or five feet. Most of the stones are in very good condition, and their inscriptions are legible. As typical in an old New England cemetery, there are many gravestones for children. Some of them are quite heartbreaking to read, such as the marker for the children of William and Polly Mordouogh. The stone tells us that they had a daughter, Adaline, who died on April 15, 1819, a month before her second birthday; a six-year-old son who died on July 27, 1819; another daughter who was only six days old and who died on June 26, 1820; and still another daughter who died September 12, 1821, not long after she was born. It is quite remarkable how families continued to try to have children after suffering so many tragic losses.

There are four doors cut into the hillside near the edge of the cemetery that lead to underground tombs. They are currently empty and quite clean, and one is currently being used for storage.

A variety of gravestones feature the nineteenth-century willow and urn motif, and each is greatly detailed. Several gravestones for children bear the carvings of newly sprouted leaves. One of these gravestones reads, "A Child of Ebenzer and Lucy Jaquith who died July 28, 1811, aged 9 days."

One of the most curious gravestones in the cemetery bears the inscription "Captain Samuel Jones' leg, which was amputated July 7, 1804." Captain Jones was an officer in the Washington town militia. While moving his house (which still stands and is located across from the general store) one day, his leg was caught between the house and a fence. The captain's leg was severely crushed and would have to be amputated, or else, Jones would face certain death. Since there was no

In Washington, the grave of Captain Samuel Jones's leg can be found. It's unknown where the rest of his body is.

anesthesia in the early nineteenth century, rum or alcohol would have been given to the captain so that he could endure the surgery. Soon after the leg was amputated and buried, the captain moved to Boston and worked at the customs house. He later moved to New York City. No one is quite sure where the rest of his body is buried, but at least we know where his leg is.

TELLING THE BEES: CAMPTON

The Pemigewasset River winds through the country village of Campton, and visitors are drawn to the area, especially to visit the scenic Blair covered bridge. There are two old cemeteries in town: Campton Village

Cemetery and Campton Hollow Cemetery. Some of the gravestones in Village Cemetery are from the early 1800s. However, more than half of the stones have been lost over the years.

During the nineteenth century, it was believed that bees held supernatural knowledge, which explains one Campton funerary tradition. If a family member who kept bees died, someone in the family had to go out to the hives and notify the bees of the death. If the bees were not informed of the death, they would abandon the hives and not return. It was also customary to drape the hives in black cloth or strips of crepe.

According to one written account, there was one family in town that did not tell the bees about the death of a family member, and the bees flew into the house, swarmed the fireplace and burned to death. Another person in Campton wrote that when her grandfather died, the bees he kept began to fly away until her grandmother draped black crepe strips over the hive. This served to "inform" the bees, and they returned back to the hive and went back to work. At another home, a man who owned several swarms of bees died, and the bees stopped working. A family member went out and told them that their master was dead and then read a chapter out of the Bible, at which point the bees went about their business. It is interesting to imagine how many times this happened, as the cemeteries in town are full of beekeeping family members.

The Grave of Old Tom Charger: Alton

Major George D. Savage was a decorated Civil War veteran who is buried in Riverside Cemetery located on Route 11 in Alton. His marker is quite easy to find in the burial ground, as it's a tall granite obelisk surrounded by a picket fence. According to the marker, he died in 1883 at the age of sixty-five and was a member of the Twelfth New Hampshire Volunteer Infantry. Over 170 men in the regiment were killed in the line of battle; another 130 died from disease.

Major Savage had returned home from the war with his charger horse, Old Tom. The major apparently had deep feelings for his faithful steed and even wanted to have the horse buried in the town's cemetery. The town compromised and had Old Tom buried just outside the cemetery gates. It certainly must have been a sight to see the large coffin containing a horse being buried in the ground.

As the cemetery expanded over the years, the grave of Old Tom ended up being part of the cemetery, and his grave can now be found right in the middle of the grounds. There is a little mound with a memorial flag that is surrounded by a white picket fence. The gravestone reads:

Here lies old Tom Charger
Ridden by Maj. Geo. D. Savage
On the Battlefields
During the Civil War

CAROLINE CUTTER'S GRAVE: MILFORD

The wordy inscription on Caroline Cutter's gravestone, located in Elm Street Cemetery in Milford, has quite a story behind it.

Caroline H.
Wife of
Calvin Cutter, MD
Murdered by the Baptist Ministry of Baptist Church as follows:
September 28, 1838, Æ 33, She was accused of Lying in Church
Meeting by the Rev. D.D. Pratt of Deacon Albert Adams. Was
condemned by the church unheard. She was reduced to poverty by
Deacon William Wallace. When an exparte [sic] council was asked
of the Milford Baptist Church by the advice of their committee, George
Raymond, Calvin Averill and Andrew Hutchinson, they voted not to
receive any communication upon the subject: The Rev. mark Carpenter
said he thought as the good old Dear Pearson said, "we have got Cutter
down and it is best to keep him down." The intentional and malicious
destruction of her character and happiness as above described destroyed
her life. Her last words were, "tell the truth."

Doctor Cutter and his wife Caroline originally lived in Nashua, New Hampshire, and they were passionate Baptists. Before the Civil War, the only Baptist church in town was located in an area known as the Heights.

Dr. Cutter and his family lived on the other side of town, and he decided that there should be a Baptist church closer to his home. Dr. Cutter was able to secure some funding for the new church but not as much as was needed. He insisted that the builders go ahead and complete the church and that they would be paid. When the church was completed, the total cost came to $33,000. Dr. Cutter did not have enough money to pay them, and the builders never received a dime. Dr. Cutter and his wife were forced out of town.

The family ended up moving in with Caroline's parents on a farm in Milford, New Hampshire. It wasn't long afterward that the family began attending the Baptist church services in Milford. Dr. Cutter decided to address the congregation at the end of services about the church in Nashua. He insisted that it was the congregation's responsibility as good Christians to pay for the Nashua church. Dr. Cutter was quite persistent, and he confronted each member of the congregation individually and demanded that they carry out their duties as Christians.

The parishioners and the church in Milford were outraged and told the doctor that he and his family were no longer allowed to attend services. While Dr. Cutter was quite upset, it was really Caroline who suffered emotionally. Caroline was told that she was not welcomed to attend any of the meetings. Strangely, she did not blame her husband; rather, she chose to blame the members of the church. To make matters worse, the couple's daughter Eliza died soon after the incident. Caroline soon became pregnant and had another child, and they named her Carrie. Caroline, however, didn't recover after the birth of her second daughter and died within a month. The doctor continued to blame the church for all of his troubles.

After Dr. Cutter commissioned his wife's gravestone, he had an announcement printed in the local paper inviting everyone to its public unveiling. Hundreds of people from Milford showed up to see the gravestone, but it did not arrive at the time Dr. Cutter had arranged. It wasn't until midnight that the stone was finally placed, and after church services the next day, nearly one thousand people came by to see the gravestone. The doctor ended up moving to Warren, Massachusetts, and remarried. Today, the gravestone stands as an emotional reminder of the Cutter family's turmoil.

South Cemetery: Portsmouth

On the corner of Sagamore Avenue and South Street is a group of burial grounds that are collectively known as South Cemetery. This is one of Portsmouth's oldest burial grounds, and the first interments are believed to have taken place during the seventeenth century. However, no records detailing these early burials exist. Auburn Cemetery, Cotton Cemetery, Proprietor's Burial Ground, Sagamore Cemetery and Harmony Grove are all a part of South Cemetery. Cotton Cemetery has some of the oldest stones to be found on the grounds, and if you are facing the cemetery from the South Street side, it is located on the left side of the cemetery.

There are literally hundreds of examples of Victorian funerary images on the gravestones. The grounds' shady lanes are canopied by tall trees, and part of the cemetery overlooks Piscataqua River inlet. In autumn, the grounds are covered in a brilliant carpet of red, gold and orange leaves. There is a wide variety of gravestones and markers throughout the area, including eighteenth-century winged skulls, an Egyptian-styled sarcophagus and several mausoleums.

Many notable people are buried in South Cemetery, including Revolutionary War soldiers, ship captains and a supreme court justice. Antethe Matea and Karen Anne Christensen, two victims of the infamous double-axe murder on Smuttynose Island off the coast of New Hampshire, were interred here in 1873. Their terrifying story inspired the book and movie *The Weight of Water*. A man named Louis Wagner was sentenced to death for the crime, but some people still wonder if perhaps a woman single-handedly committed the murders and managed to escape.

The grave marker of robber baron Frank Jones can easily be found as it's the tallest in the cemetery (and in the state of New Hampshire). This monument is twenty-eight feet tall, and Jones had it commissioned about twenty years before he died. Jones's brewery, named (of course) Frank Jones Brewery, was once the largest brewery in the United States. Many of the buildings still stand in various states of disrepair on nearby Islington Street. Jones also owned the Wentworth by the Sea Hotel, a grand hotel that was built during New Castle's golden age. In addition, Frank Jones was mayor of Portsmouth for two terms. He ran for governor but lost by only two thousand votes. Jones was

Photograph of South Cemetery in Portsmouth. Before the cemetery was constructed, the site served as a place of execution.

also a congressman for several terms. These ventures afforded him the opportunity to build and purchase property throughout Portsmouth and the surrounding areas, and there are well over one hundred buildings in the area that Jones commissioned.

He is interred with his brother Hiram, who committed suicide by slitting his throat in the privy on the family farm in Barrington. Frank married Hiram's pregnant wife, Martha, after his death, and there are rumors that the child may actually have been Frank's and that Hiram may have met with foul play, but there is no concrete proof.

It is worth noting that the cemetery was once used as an execution ground, and many hangings were held here during the eighteenth century. The 1768 execution of Ruth Blay is one of the well known executions that took place in South Cemetery. Ruth Blay was a twenty-five-year-old schoolteacher from Hampton who was carrying the illegitimate child of one of the men in town. After delivering the stillborn child herself, she was so distraught and frightened of the consequences that she buried the baby beneath the floorboards of the school. One of Ruth's students witnessed the incident, and the child thought that Ruth murdered her baby. The child ran home to tell her parents. Ruth was indicted for concealing the death of an illegitimate child, but she was not charged for murder since there was no evidence that the child had been killed or was stillborn. She was quickly found guilty and sentenced to death by hanging. Although several reprieves were issued to halt the execution, she was finally sentenced to hang on December 31, 1768.

Sheriff Packer, who was presiding over Ruth's hanging, received word that a final governor's reprieve was being issued. The documentation, however, was slow to arrive, and the sheriff had already planned to have his dinner on time that day. The sheriff refused to wait any longer for the pardon to arrive and insisted that the hanging take place at the designated hour. Ruth was brought to the scaffold by cart, and a large crowd had assembled to witness her end. People in the crowd implored Sheriff Packer to wait for the pardon to arrive, much to Sheriff Packer's annoyance. At exactly noon, the sheriff ordered the cart to be drawn away. Ruth's body twisted in the chilly December air, and the crowd watched in disbelief. A few minutes later, a messenger on horseback carrying the pardon from the governor rode up and placed the paperwork in the hand of Sheriff Packer. Disgusted by the actions of the sheriff, the townspeople assembled later that day and marched over toward his house. The angry mob burned an effigy of him on the lawn and shouted all sorts of angry and foul sentiments.

Despite the outcry and anger of the people, Packer remained sheriff for a few more years and died quite wealthy. His body is buried in North Cemetery in Portsmouth. Ruth Blay was quietly buried in an unmarked grave near the cemetery pond. A few years after her death, the State of New Hampshire abolished the death penalty.

The tale was memorialized in the "Ballad of Ruth Blay," published in Thomas Bailey Aldrich's *An Old Town By The Sea*. The following is an excerpt:

> *When at last, in tones of warning,*
> *From its high and airy tower,*
> *Slowly with its tongue of iron,*

Tolled the bell the fatal hour;
Like the sound of distant billows,
When the storm is wild and loud,
Breaking on the rocky headland,
Ran a murmur through the crowd.
And a voice among them shouted,
"Pause before the deed is done;

We have asked reprieve and pardon
For the poor misguided one."
But these words of Sheriff Packer
Rang above the swelling noise:
"Must I wait and lose my dinner?
Draw away the cart, my boys!"

Nearer came the sound and louder,
Till a steed with panting breath,
From its sides the white foam dripping,
Halted at the scene of death;

And a messenger alighted,
Crying to the crowd, "Make way!
This I bear to Sheriff Packer;
'Tis a pardon for Ruth Blay!"

South Cemetery is rumored to be one of the most haunted locations in Portsmouth. Shadow people are said to wander the grounds during and after sunset. The shadow people are believed to be protective spirits that watch over the spirits of the dead. A local resident related that one evening, while she was walking through the cemetery, she sensed a spirit walking with her. She kept turning around to see if anyone else was there, but she never saw anyone. Disturbed, she quickly got into her car and drove home. She claimed that the spirit followed her from the cemetery to her house, as she could still sense a presence. The woman was so frightened that she called a local psychic to come to her house and send the spirit away.

The graveyard is large enough that you can easily spend several days exploring the grounds and visiting the many graves, mausoleums and family burial plots. Two gravestones near the pond are said to glow inexplicably late at night. The graves do not face the nearby road, so it's impossible that the glow is the reflected light from the headlights of passing cars or streetlights. According to reports, this phenomenon is best viewed from the highest part of the hill. Some have claimed seeing a dark figure standing behind the glowing stones as well.

Many visitors to the cemetery have brought cameras to photograph this phenomenon and any wandering apparitions. Others have attempted to make contact with the dead through Ouija boards. Many people believe they have captured not only images of orbs but full-bodied apparitions at South Cemetery. A handful of people have reported seeing a blue lady walking towards the center of the cemetery.

Chapter Seven
Unearthing the Ghosts

HALLOWEEN HAUNTS: ACWORTH

If you can find your way to Old Acworth Cemetery, you might just have to consider yourself related to the great mapmaker Ferdinand Magellan. It can be a challenging place to find, as there are very few roads that lead to Acworth, and if you miss your turn, you will soon find that you are miles and miles from where you had hoped to be.

According to a recent census, fewer than one thousand people live in this rural village. The town was incorporated in 1772 and started out as a collection of just thirteen houses. Soon, a few small mills were established, and the town grew.

During the Centennial Celebration in 1872, the festivities were marred by a fierce storm that blew in just as the celebration was getting underway. Everyone scattered and took shelter inside their homes. Instead of celebrating outside, the townspeople stayed inside, reminisced and shared stories and songs about the past and future. One song lyric references those who have passed on:

The dew falls here in tears at eve
On graves of those we love
And we who at their stillness grieve
Keep watch and ward above

The trees in Old Acworth Cemetery stand guard over the dead who have been buried there for over two hundred years.

Center Cemetery was officially established in 1776, and the grounds encompass some of the most textured landscape in the area. The stories from this cemetery are as creepy as a nighttime walk through the stones. There are a variety of broken and overgrown stones in the cemetery, but the memory of the dead seems to vibrate in the wind as it bends the long ferns over old stones. The trees add much to the mood of the cemetery as well. If you look closely at the textured bark, you can make out facial features and fingers. Is it just something in the soil, or is it the fact that the roots of the tree have buried themselves so deep that they are now taking on the images of the dead?

The gravestone for Deacon Jonathan Silsby reads:

From apparent health instantly expired
on Sabbath noon, Jan. 2, 1820,
after leaving the Lord's table
where he had just served. 70y

Another gravestone tells of a time when dead bodies were used for scientific research. The business of obtaining cadavers for research was popular in big cities and small towns alike. As it happened, on October 31, 1824, Bezaleel Beckwith died at the age of forty-three, and his remains were buried in the Old Acworth Cemetery. Thirteen days after he was buried, his grave was robbed.

Immediately, people were suspicious that medical students from Dartmouth may have committed the crime. However, according to records, a man named James Wilson Jr. of Acworth was arrested in Castleton, Vermont, and he was charged with stealing the body for dissection. Wilson was brought back to Acworth to stand trial for the crime, and his bail was set at $700. Strangely, the case never went to trial, and the bail was forfeited. Despite Wilson's arrest, many of the townsfolk continued to believe that the medical students at Dartmouth had a hand in the robbery.

The gravestone that was commissioned by Beckwith's friends reads:

This stone tells of the death of Bezaleel Beckwith,
not where his body lies.
He died Oct. 31, 1824 age 43.
The thirteenth day after his body was stolen from the grave.
Now twice bereaved the mourner cries
My friend is dead, his body gone,
God's act is just my heart replies,
Forgive, oh God, what man has done.

According to local legend, Halloween night is an especially frightening night to be wandering the old cemetery. Many people have reported seeing an apparition at the grave of Bezaleel on Halloween. The ghost is rumored to be Bezaleel, who comes back every Halloween because his spirit cannot rest in peace. Visitors who have gone looking for a ghostly experience on Halloween night say that they have not been disappointed.

Beebe Cemetery: Star Island, Isles of Shoals

About nine miles off the New Hampshire coast is a group of islands known as the Isles of Shoals. The isles were first discovered in the late 1500s by Captain John Smith and were named because of their resemblance to a school (or shoal) of fish. Many mysterious and fantastic tales of pirates, buried treasure and, of course, ghosts have been told about the islands.

In 1873, John Poore joined a group of homes and established the Oceanic Hotel. The beautiful view and the cool ocean breezes attracted summer visitors from as far south as New York. After a fire in 1875, the property was rebuilt and served as a hotel for several years; however, interest waned in the late nineteenth century, as new resorts began to spring up all over the White Mountains. In 1900, the property became a religious retreat and has been used for that purpose ever since.

There is a small family cemetery located just behind the hotel where the graves of the three Beebe children can be found. Reverend George Beebe moved his family to the island in 1857 so that he could minister to the people there, and he also served as the local doctor until 1869. Sadly, in 1863, Reverend Beebe's son, Mitty, contracted an infectious disease from the school on the mainland. His two sisters also fell ill, and the three of them died within weeks of each other.

The marble stone has lost its luster over the years, but some of the touching inscriptions on the obelisk are still legible:

Mitty, Died Jun. 23, 1863, age 7
"I don't want to die, but I'll do just as Jesus wants me to."

His sister Millie's inscription reads:

Died Jun. 12, 1863
Age 4 years
"Dying she kneeled down and prayed:
Please Jesus, take me up to the Lighted Place. And HE did"

The inscription for little Jessie Beebe is hard to decipher, but her name, age (two) and death date (May 30, 1863) are clear. The reverend moved to Littleton, New Hampshire, in 1867, and the four surviving children who lived on the island sold their land to John Poore, who established the hotel a few years later.

The three headstones for the children are located just to the right of the obelisk. The fence that once surrounded the cemetery disappeared some years ago, and the cemetery itself was overrun with ivy and brambles that completely obscured the graves. For years, people who visited the island reported seeing two little girls and a boy who fit the age and description of the Beebe children playing near the cemetery. When approached, they would run into the brambles by the cemetery and disappear. Laughter and soft voices have also been heard emanating from the cemetery.

A few years ago, volunteers and members of the Star Island Corporation undertook the task of cleaning and maintaining the cemetery grounds. And while the cemetery is no longer wild with overgrown weeds and vines, the spirits of the three children are still said to romp nearby.

KEEPING THE WITCH IN THE GRAVE: EAST ALTON

Alton is a little town that is located on a bay and is part of Lake Winnipesaukee. Originally settled in 1770, it has become a summer vacation destination for many who enjoy the beauty and recreation of the lake. Hidden away in an isolated part of East Alton is the Glidden family cemetery. The cemetery is difficult to find as it lies in between two homes on private property. There are some broken stones in the cemetery, and it appears that there are no visitors who tread there.

Sarah Glidden, who is buried in this cemetery, died in 1825 at the age of forty-two. Church records state that "Brother Moses Glidden's wife was killed by a stream of lightning. The shock was solemn and awful. The people appeared awakened and many who had not prayed many years began to pray the following evening. Her remains were committed to the house for all living on the Sabbath after in presence of a very solemn assembly."

Many superstitious people in town believed that Sarah was struck down by God for being a witch and for not attending church services.

According to the story, the day she was killed by the lightning was a clear, sunny day. Apparently, Sarah had no interest in going to church; rather, she preferred to work in her fields, and her actions inspired much speculation about her beliefs and lifestyle.

Her manner of burial confirmed for many that she was, indeed, a witch. A long rock slab was placed over her coffin, which according to legend, was placed there to keep her from rising out of the grave and bewitching and tormenting others. Some people believe that the stone has nothing to do with witchcraft and that it was simply put there to keep the animals from rooting and digging into the graves, as they were allowed to roam freely about the town at one time. However, Sarah's grave was (and still is) the only grave in the area that had a stone slab over the coffin, and that was enough for many to think she was a witch.

OLD CENTER CEMETERY: ANDOVER

Old Center Cemetery was established in 1780. The land was given to Benjamin Cilley as a place to bury the town's dead. There are many unmarked graves in the cemetery, and the oldest stones are unmarked fieldstone markers. Some of the notable graves in the cemetery are mentioned in the town's history books:

> *While a body of troops was marching through Andover towards the northern during the War of 1812. Three soldiers were taken sick. One was left at tavern at Kimball's corner one at Benjamin Thompson's tavern and one the tavern of Moses Johnson in West Andover. The name of one was unknown another Asa was the only name that could be learned while the third at Kimball's was Hiram Hill of Maine. They all died and were buried in the northwest of the old cemetery at the Center.*

There are many paupers of the town who are also buried in the cemetery. According to town records, there was a specific procedure in place to deal with people who were unfortunate or, in some cases, just simply lazy. According to the *History of the Town of Andover*:

The Old Center Cemetery in Andover is a very eerie place to visit after dark when ghosts are said to roam.

Among the conditions pertaining to the sale and care of paupers in 1820 were the following items. Each person will be struck off to the lowest bidder for the term of one year. Any person bidding off a pauper shall furnish him or her with suitable meats drinks and clothing nursing if sick and every accommodation which is necessary for their support doctors bills excepted.

Documents in reference to a pauper's sale in 1820 contained the following information:

Mr Frasure sold to Ebenezer Tilton at $1.00 per week
Widow Hannah Rano to Henry D Hilton at $.56 per week
Eliza Meloon to Timothy Swett at $0.35 per week
Samuel Sleeper to Samuel Cilley at $0.90 per week
Widow H Gove to Jonathan Martin at $0.10 per week
The York child to Joseph Sevey at $0.50 per week

The remaining stones, for the most part, are severely weathered, and they display a variety of lichens and long black streaks on both sides of the stones. The cemetery is especially eerie after the sun goes down. Of course, that is when the ghosts are said to come out and play. There have been numerous sightings of a ghostly woman wearing a long dress in the far corner of the cemetery. There are also rumors that a ghost of a man who made a deal with the devil wanders the cemetery, desperately reaching out from the darkness to get the attention of the living.

For those curious souls who are interested in spirit photography, the cemetery seems to be a hotspot for orbs, light anomalies and shadow people.

The Ghosts of Meetinghouse Cemetery: Antrim

Meetinghouse Cemetery is located at the top of a high dusty hill in Antrim. First laid out in 1777, just eleven years after the town was settled, the cemetery is the resting place for many of those who first cleared the land to build the village. Most of the first settlers were of Scotch-Irish descent. Many believe that the spirits in the cemetery that wander the grounds are searching for peace and comfort.

While there are many old slate gravestones to be found, the cemetery has a large amount of gravestones that bear the date 1800, and most of these gravestones belong to children. The stone-carved faces remind passersby of the terrible suffering of the families and community of Antrim. The summer of 1800 was described as very hot and dry—perfect conditions to support an outbreak of dysentery. The first death happened on July 23, and by September 23, sixty-nine people had died, most of whom were children. According to records, nineteen funerals were held in one week in August alone, and almost every single day during those two months, another funeral was held. Many families lost all of their children, and the total number of deaths made up one-fifteenth of the entire population.

There are a large number of unmarked graves for children who died in the 1800 epidemic. The cemetery is believed to be haunted, and the ghosts are said to belong to the children who died from dysentery that summer. The incidents and experiences that people have described are

There are several gravestones for the children who died in the dysentery epidemic of 1800. Most of these graves, however, were not marked.

quite fascinating. People have reported feeling small invisible hands reach out and tug at their clothing or grasp their hands, almost as if seeking reassurance and company. Local paranormal groups have reported seeing child-like apparitions wandering the cemetery at night.

VALE END CEMETERY: WILTON

According to Anna Fiske's gravestone, located in Vale End Cemetery, "All is well." However, there are many who believe all is not well in what is considered to be one of the most haunted cemeteries in the granite state. From its beginnings, the town of Wilton has had its share of historical tragedies. In 1773, the townsfolk decided that a meetinghouse should be built. In April that year, the town voted that six barrels of rum, a barrel of brown sugar, half a box of lemons and two loaves of sugar would be furnished to the men who would be raising the building.

On September 7, many gathered to celebrate the meetinghouse's groundbreaking. But just a few hours later, joy turned into horror when the central support beam of the building broke loose. Fifty-three men fell thirty feet to the ground and were buried underneath heavy beams and tons of building material. At the end of the day, five men were dead and many others were permanently injured. The town undertook a second attempt at building a meetinghouse, but that building also collapsed, and so did several others. Finally, a meetinghouse was completed, but not long after, a fire erupted during a community dance, and many barely escaped with their lives.

One of the resident ghosts is known as the "Blue Lady," and she is purported to be the spirit of a woman who was known as Mary Ritter Spaulding. According to records, Mary gave birth to seven children between 1795, the year she was married, and 1808, the year she died. Paranormal investigators who have claimed to have spoken to Mary state that she bore an eighth child in 1807, although there are no records of this child's existence. Many believe that her intense grief over losing the child is what ties her restless spirit to this earth. According to another theory, she remains earthbound because she was buried with her husband's second wife. A blue shaft of light is said to surround her form, and she seems to float in midair. There are countless numbers of paranormal groups who have claimed to have both seen and communicated with her.

Mary's tall, broken gravestone can be found at the edge of the cemetery, in the back corner near the pine trees. Trinkets or gifts are often placed around her stone by those who believe her spirit roams the area.

Gnomes, or "puckwudgies," are also believed to roam the edges of Vale End. Puckwudgies are believed to be linked to Native American lore, and these creatures are rumored to have the ability to shape-shift into other beings and can appear and disappear at will. Whether or not these reports are true, local police officers regularly patrol the area at night in order to keep curiosity seekers away from the grounds and away from shape-shifting gnomes or the Blue Lady.

Pine Hill Cemetery: Hollis

Some ghost stories are so blown out of proportion that it is often difficult to separate fact from fiction.

The specters that roam Pine Hill Cemetery in the town of Hollis may have good reason to. Locals refer to the cemetery as Blood Cemetery, and that name conjures up all sorts of images. The reason why some refer to it as Blood Cemetery is due to the fact that members of the Blood family are buried there. The gravestone of Abel Blood tells us that he died at the age of seventy in 1867, and his wife Betsy died in 1827 at the age of twenty-six. It also notes that their son George died in 1830 at the age of three. The upward pointed finger engraved on the tombstone allegedly changes direction at night, pointing towards the ground. The family's history is void of tragedy, and rumors that they were involved with the occult seem to be quite untrue. In fact, Abel was described as a good Christian man.

Many have reported strange sights and sounds in the cemetery. Recently, however, various stones in the cemetery have been vandalized. The gravestone for Abel was broken off and has disappeared, and numerous toppled stones can be found along the hillside.

Still, many people are not deterred by the frequent police patrols or the motion sensors that have been placed on the hallowed grounds to protect the dead from the living. There seems to be no shortage of people who want to visit the site themselves and find out if the legends are really true. The closest thing to a ghost story the cemetery has to offer is the tale of the ghost of a little boy who jumps out at passersby. Perhaps they should heed the message of this wandering spirit and allow those buried here to remain at rest.

Gilson Road Cemetery: Nashua

The small roadside burial ground known as Gilson Road Cemetery is a fairly small cemetery. Most of the gravestones date to the nineteenth century, and just a few are from the twentieth century. There are many unmarked graves littered throughout the grounds.

Many people believe Gilson Road Cemetery to be one of the most haunted locations in the state.

Members of the Gilson, Fisk and Robbins families are interred in the cemetery. The gravestones are not terribly notable; many are made of slate bearing the willow and urn motif. There is a small marker that reads: "Baby Gilson. Often little gifts or offerings are left on top of the gravestones. An abundance of pennies can often be found right at the entrance gate."

This cemetery is allegedly a hotbed for ghost activity, making it a popular spot among paranormal investigators. Novice and experienced ghost hunters alike have collected photographs of orbs and light anomalies here. Many investigators from paranormal groups claim that there are multiple spirits that frequent these grounds, and these spirits can often be seen in the back of the cemetery near the stone wall.

While it appears to be a fairly peaceful cemetery, there are many who say it is anything but quiet.

Center Burying Ground: Henniker

According to the town's history, Henniker was established in 1761 and only had one family. By 1775, the town's population had grown to 367. At a town meeting on March 26, 1770, it was decided that a cemetery was needed. The record reads: "Voted that the burying place shall be upon the Senter lot. Voted that Josiar Ward Ezra tucker Silas Barns is a Com to lok out the spot of ground to bury the Ded in. Voted that Josiar Ward should dig the graves this year."

The general health of the population was attributed to the town's clean air, good water and spaciousness. Many gravestones throughout the cemetery reveal residents lived long lives; a few denote that some residents lived to be one hundred years old. In 1838, Reverend Jacob Scales wrote:

> *The town has been usually very healthy and the average number of deaths has been about one to sixty inhabitants. Very many of the inhabitants have lived to more than eighty years and some more than ninety. Industry and frugality appear to have been the leading traits in the character of every one who has in this place reached the age of ninety years.*

The Center Burying Ground is also the final resting place for one of Henniker's most famous residents—Mary Wilson Wallace. According to the story, Mary was born at sea aboard the ship *Wolf*, just outside of Boston harbor on July 28, 1720. This ship was captured by the pirate Don Pedro, who was known for being quite ruthless. Pedro could have killed everyone on the ship and taken it for himself, but when he learned that there was a newborn child on board, he changed his mind. He asked Elizabeth Fulton-Wilson if she would name her newborn daughter after his beloved mother, and if she did, he would let the ship go. Mrs. Wilson hastily agreed, and Don Pedro left the ship, returning one final time carrying gifts. One of the gifts he brought was a bolt of beautiful green Chinese silk, and he asked that when Mary was old enough, a wedding gown be made for her out of the fabric.

Not long after the ship arrived in Boston, Mr. Wilson died, and his widow and daughter continued to Londonderry, New Hampshire. Mrs.

Wilson settled into Londonderry and eventually remarried. Mary was described as being very tall, with long red flowing hair and a wonderful personality. She also reportedly had elegant manners and spoke with a distinct Scottish brogue.

In December of 1742, "Ocean-Born Mary" (as she had come to be known) married Scottish immigrant James Wallace, and they had four children. Mary's wedding gown was made out of the Chinese silk that Don Pedro had given to her mother. Today, a piece of her wedding dress is in the Henniker Town Library. Ocean-Born Mary died on February 13, 1814 and is buried in the cemetery behind Henniker's original town hall.

Mary Wilson Wallace's grave is easy to find and is about halfway down the central path in the cemetery. The stone bears a willow and urn, and there is a small plaque at the base of the stone that reads, "Ocean Born Mary." The inscription on the slate says, "In Memory of Widow Mary Wallace who died Feby 13 1814 in the 94th year of her age."

This quiet cemetery on the edge of a hill offers beautiful foliage in the fall, and the large stone wall that borders the front of the grounds adds a distinct New England charm. Two giant pine trees stand like sentinels at the entrance gates to the cemetery, and their thick roots extend throughout the grounds and most likely into the coffins that lie underground. A small white building near the right-hand corner of the cemetery was built in 1842, and at one time, stored the town hearse.

Many people believe the burial ground is haunted, and some say that Ocean-Born Mary is the ghost. According to one legend from the late 1960s, two police officers saw a spirit rise from Mary's grave, climb aboard a phantom carriage and ride across town. Some people claim to have felt the presence of a spirit while standing by her grave. Curious visitors attempting to make contact with her spirit through electronic devices describe recording whispers and knocking sounds at her grave, and they maintain that there was no logical explanation for the noise.

Strangely enough, stories of Mary's ghost do not stop at the graveyard; some people believe that her house was haunted as well. Auguste Roy of Wisconsin purchased the house that Mary lived in during her time in Henniker, and he opened it up for tours. He invited those who believed in ghosts to come inside and hear all of the unusual tales of paranormal

Does the spirit of "Ocean-Born Mary" rise from the grave and travel across the town of Henniker on Halloween?

activity. He claimed a rocking chair by the fireplace rocked on its own and that one could feel Mary standing next to the hearth. He also said that Mary could be seen at the top of the staircase in the house. The house was even investigated by Dr. Hans Holzer, a paranormal expert, who agreed that the house was haunted.

The story of Ocean-Born Mary has never really died; books are still written about her to this day. For many people, her story has turned into an extravagant legend. Other people strongly believe that her fiery spirit still wanders the grounds of the town she called home.

An Unusual Burial: Barnstead

A very strange tale from 1812 is related in Barnstead's town history book. Workers who were clearing the area to build a new road came across a skeleton buried in a shallow grave. On closer inspection of the remains, the townsfolk determined that the person had been murdered and that the murderer quickly buried the body to hide the deed.

Instead of burying the body in the town cemetery, the body was placed underneath the steps of the Parade Church, where it could be viewed in part by passersby. The thought was that someone who passed the remains might feel the weight of their guilt, come forward and confess. For a year, the townspeople endured the rotting corpse and all of the nightmares it inspired. There were even stories that dying groans emanated from the remains, and some people believed that the spirit of the dead man hovered around the moldering bones.

Nearly a year after the corpse was placed underneath the steps, a woman from another town said that her husband, who was headed to Barnstead, disappeared around the time of the murder. The bones were given to her, much to the relief of the townspeople.

Shadow People of the Hidden Cemetery: Durham

Durham, New Hampshire, was originally settled as The Oyster River Plantation in 1635. The name came from the discovery of a large bed of oysters halfway between the falls and mouth of the river. Initially part of Dover, the town was incorporated as Durham in 1736. Today, the town is home to the University of New Hampshire.

In July 1694, during King Philip's War, the village was savagely attacked by the French and Abenaki Indians. That late-night sneak attack against the villagers was swift, and they didn't have a chance. All five of their garrisons were burned to the ground, along with their crops. Approximately 104 of the villagers were killed, and another 27 were taken captive. Many of the villagers were tortured and scalped, and their homes were burned. The church, however, was spared, as the minister is said to have written religious verses on the wall in hopes God would intervene. It took years for the village to recover from the devastating raid.

Located along the banks of the Oyster River, the Three Chimneys Inn and Ffrost Sawyer Tavern affords visitors a fine view of terraced gardens and waterways. Valentine Hill built and owned a sawmill and a gristmill along the falls of the river, and the sawmill helped to expand Durham's shipbuilding trade. Valentine Hill was then granted five hundred acres for a farm adjacent to his sawmill. His home was built in 1649 and was brought up the river by gundalow. It was a single-story house with a basement and an upstairs living area with a combined kitchen. This part of the house is now the Ffrost Sawyer Tavern. The home was part of the original village settlement and is the oldest house in Durham (and one of the oldest in New Hampshire).

Behind the tavern is an old cemetery that is almost as old as the house itself. The cemetery is hard to spot, unless you know where to look for it; it's shrouded underneath the tall pine trees. The cemetery features an underground tomb, fieldstone grave markers from the early 1700s and some slanted, weather-worn marble gravestones.

The tavern itself is the setting for several ghost stories that have been documented over the years. A former employee at the tavern was completely convinced the property was haunted. He said that when he often left the tavern for the night, he would look down the hill toward the cemetery and see shadows of people moving around in the graveyard. The parking lot would always be empty, and there was no one around. The shadow people who moved about the gravestones are familiar to many, and the few reported sightings are enough to keep the especially superstitious away.

While most of the ghostly incidents are said to happen in the fall, the old cemetery definitely has an air of mystery about it, especially given that it lies at the bottom of a hill below a well-known haunted tavern. Should you decide to pay a visit to the tavern (and do not run into the haunting spirit of Hannah Sawyer, a young lady who committed suicide), you may want to venture out to the cemetery after dark—but only if you dare. Some people believe that the ghosts in the cemetery might be spirits of people who were killed in the brutal Indian raid of 1694.

Chapter Eight
Speaking Stones: Epitaphs to Remember

MEETINGHOUSE CEMETERY (OLD CENTER CEMETERY): MARLBOROUGH

Most of the gravestones in this old burial ground are in very good condition, and many date back to the eighteenth century. But what makes this cemetery intriguing is the long row of above-ground tombs that borders one area of the grounds. Below is a selection of gravestones that bear moving epitaphs.

Sarah, wife of Samuel Taggard
Died
Feb. 17, 1855
Ae. 68 yrs.
Our mother taught us love
And how to live and die.

Mrs. Lois Relict of
The late Lt. Oliver Wright
Died
Feb. 25, 1837
Ae. 92
She expired beneath the roof
with her 5th generation

Ripe for heaven.
Erected by Mrs. Lydia Wright

In memory of Mr. Joseph Haskell
Who Died
Jan. 7, 1825
Ae. 55
Weep not my loving friends for me
For I've gone to Eternity
The ways of death you all must tread
And sleep with me amongst the dead.

In memory of Achsah, dau. of
Mr. Elijah and Mrs. Dorcas Gates
Died
Sept. 8, 1800
Ae. 2 yrs. 8 mos.
Youth like a vernal flower appears
Most promising and fair
But death like an untimely frost
Puts all in silence there.

Patty Ward
5ᵗʰ dau. Of Capt. Reuben and Mrs. Sally Ward
Died
Nov. 14, 1795
Ae. 5 yrs. 6 mo. 27 days
By boiling cider she was burned
Whilst less than six of age
Then her exquisite racking pain
Removed her from the stage
To the Almighty King
Where all the godly ones are sent
The praise of God to sing.

Pine Ridge Cemetery: Hancock

Hancock is a sleepy little town that is located along the Contoocook River. The town, named for John Hancock, was first settled in 1764. Hancock Village has changed little over the past one hundred years; old gravel paths still lead from building to building.

The lovely Pine Ridge Cemetery is the oldest burial place in town and is located just off the town common. The metal row numbers that are fastened to the stone wall on both sides of the ground are an unusual cemetery feature. Beneath each row letter is a marker, and each marker has its own rusty patina. Nearly all of these markers are still intact.

The variety of ironwork and gravestone art found in the cemetery can keep one busy for hours. In the center of the cemetery are two plots that are surrounded by an ornately shaped iron fence featuring willow trees and lambs. Another plot is surrounded by four iron posts, each bearing an iron tassel, signifying the drawing of life's curtain or the closing of the mourning shroud.

A survey and transcription of the cemetery conducted in 1910 revealed that there were 950 gravestones and 1,034 inscriptions. Some of these stones are now gone, but there are still many that reflect the beliefs of the town's earliest residents.

The gravestone for Mary E., wife of Joseph Simonds, is especially striking. According to the inscription, Mary died on January 23, 1849. The stone also lists Samuel W., the couple's only son, who died on January 24, 1849. He was only two days old. Swirling spirals decorate the top and side borders of the stone, while the inner design depicts a woman lying on a bed with a small child at her side. Even after 150 years, the stone is still in wonderful condition. Behind the row of gravestones where Mary Simonds lies are hundreds of lily of the valley flowers, which were popular in the nineteenth century and were known as "the ladder of heaven."

Following is a selection of some of the very poignant epitaphs in Pine Ridge Cemetery.

Willow trees and lambs are featured in the beautifully detailed fence around the Greenwood family.

This gravestone for Mary Simonds depicts Mary lying behind a curtain with her child by her side.

MARY A.
Wife of Joshua Foster
DIED
May 28, 1851
Aged 48 Years
Here lies a mother and her only daughter,
Closed in the grave,
Side by side
With hopes of meeting
Their precious Saviour.

William Robinson
Born Jan. 14, 1814
DIED
Apr. 9, 1895
There shall be no night there.

David Moors
Died
Sept. 15, 1841
AE 29
Here peacefully lies the once happy father
The joy of his beloved wife and daughter
But whilst in health
The woodsman axe he sped,
God aimed the tree and crushed him dead.

Neverson Greenwood
DIED
Feb. 22, 1845
AE 33
Leaves have their time to fall
And flowers to wither at the north
Winds breath
And stars to set, but all
Thou hast all season for thine own, O Death.

Erected to the memory of
Mrs. Hannah Hills
Wife of Mr. Joseph Hills
Who died
Aug. 2, 1822
Though greedy worms devour my skin,
and gnaw my wasting flesh,
when God shall build my bones again
He'll doth them all afresh
Then shall I see thy lovely face
With strong Immortal eyes
And feast upon thy unknown grace
With pleasure and surprise.

Jack Ware
An African died
March 2, 1826
Aged about 100 years
This monument erected in
Commemoration of his virtues
By the voluntary contributions
Of the citizens of Hancock.

The largest marker in the cemetery bears the image of a coffin near the bottom. It reads:

Miss Ruth Knight
Daughter of Enos & Dorcus Knight
Died Oct. 30, 1816
AE 24 years
Escap'd from death. O safe
On that calm shore.
Where sin & pain and passion are no more.
Lo soft remembrance drops a pious tear,
And sacred friendship sits a mourner here.

Should you decide to visit Hancock, you might want to stop by the historical society, which is located at 7 Main Street, just a short walk away from the cemetery. One of the historical society's treasured artifacts is an item known as the "Town Coffin." The coffin was a temporary coffin for those died and whose family could not afford to purchase a coffin. Once the deceased had been interred, the coffin would be reused. Additionally, the coffin was to hold a dead body during the winter months, when the ground was too frozen to dig a grave. There was a short period where the coffin was not in the town's possession; the coffin somehow fell into the hands of a local farmer named Guy Stover, who used it to store chicken feed. Ruth Johnson, the town historian at the time, wanted the coffin back, as it was an important historic artifact. So Ruth had her husband, Willis, construct a grain bin for Stover and exchanged it for the old coffin.

CHESTER VILLAGE CEMETERY: CHESTER

There is a historical sign just outside of the gates of the village cemetery in Chester, New Hampshire, that reads:

> *This graveyard, one of the oldest in the state, was purchased by Col. John Blunt for 70 pounds in 1751. Signed stones by the finest stone sculptors in New England are found here. Among these craftsmen are: Stephen and Abel Webster, John Marble, John Wright and Timothy Eastman. Revolutionary heroes rest here as well as two governors of the state, Samuel and John Bell, William Richardson, Chief Justice of the N.H. Supreme Court, Isaac Blasdel the clockmaker, and others.*

The cemetery, located at the junction of Route 121 and 102 in Chester, is one of two cemeteries in New Hampshire that are on the National Register of Historic Places.

The cemetery's older section features a wonderful variety of gravestones with a wide variety of carvings. Some of the stones feature engravings of human faces that are solemn and expressionless. There are others that feature smiling faces; others depict frowning persons. There are simple, primitive-style stones and fieldstone markers scattered about

Chester Village Cemetery has an eighteenth-century section that features a wide variety of carving styles and images.

the cemetery as well. If you look closely at some of the gravestones, you may find a tiny inscription that reveals who carved it.

For example, at the very bottom of Hannah Webster's gravestone, behind the blades of grass, is a tiny inscription that reads, "Stephen Webster of Holles 1762." Stephen Webster was the stone's carver, and many of his stones and those carved by his brother, Abel, can be found throughout southern New Hampshire. Stephen often carved frowning faces on his gravestones while Abel carved more cheerful, smiling faces. It was rumored that the difference in style reflected the Websters' feelings about death. Others believed that the faces represented what each brother felt was the fate of the deceased.

In analyzing the brothers' different styles, the New Hampshire Historical Society suggested that their gravestones might have been painted. The gravestones in Chester bear traces of what appear to be black and red pigment. The black pigment is only seen in the deep letters of the carvings. The concept that the gravestones may actually have been painted alludes to how striking their stones may actually have been.

At the bottom of the gravestone for Hannah Webster is the signature of the stone carver.

The gravestone for Eleanor Colby features an upside-down coffin and heart to symbolize the mortal remains interred in the ground.

According to Harriette Merrifield Forbes's book *Gravestones of Early New England and the Men Who Made Them, 1653–1800* (1966), the "traces of color on these stones suggest a new image of eighteenth century mortuary art, and should alert researchers elsewhere to the possible uses of paint in early graveyards."

During the autumn months, the leaves on the maple trees begin to turn colors and fall to the ground, covering up the small piles of broken gravestones that are hidden behind the trees. Sadly, the stones crumble away a little more each year. But visitors can enjoy what remains as they wander the cemetery's new walkways.

West Claremont (Union) Cemetery: Claremont

On March 29, 1768, the town of Claremont voted to "take two acres of land off the northwest corner of the fair for a burying ground." The reason why this cemetery is known as both West Claremont Cemetery and Union Cemetery is because the Union Church sits across the street. (It also happens to be the oldest standing Episcopal church in New Hampshire, dating back to 1773.)

The cemetery is a treasure-trove of fascinating epitaphs and very unusual carvings. Many of the gravestones in the cemetery actually detail the manner in which the interred died. Below is one example.

> *Here lies buried Mr. Joel Roys who*
> *Fell in to a Fier* [sic]
> *And burnt to death*
> *Sept 4ᵗʰ 1782*
> *In the 27ᵗʰ year of his age.*
> *O! Mortality*

Joel Roys's granddaughter shared the circumstances surrounding Joel's death in an interview. One night, Joel was lighting a pile of logs when they suddenly came loose and began to roll towards him, knocking him down. He was pinned beneath them in a matter of seconds. His wife tried to assist him, but she couldn't move the burning logs, and all of the men in the town were at a meeting, so no one was able to help

This gravestone from 1798 features two sad faces in reference to the two children that are buried there. One was only three days old at the time of death, and the other was only five hours old.

William Whiting's grave in Claremont, New Hampshire.

Left: The gravestone for David Ives in Claremont depicts a very unusual profile of an angel and flower.

Below: Esther Hitchock's grave features a crescent moon, stars, coffin on legs, willow branch and what appears to be an apple.

Daniel Ashley's gravestone states that he died in 1810 with a "cancer on his face."

her. Joel was a Revolutionary War soldier who served three years in the military.

Another tombstone describes the death of two little boys:

Sacred to the memory
of Zara and Orlando Thomas,
sons of Zara and Elizabeth
Thomas. They were killed with
lightning July 8, 1805,
Zara in his 18th year, Orlando in his 7th year

According to the story, the two boys were standing in an open doorway during a very severe thunderstorm that had blown through town. An old musket hung above the doorway, and it was believed that it had attracted the lightning that killed the two boys into the room. The lightning also hit a table and took out one very long, single sliver of wood.

Following are a few of the other interesting epitaphs that can be found in the cemetery:

In Memory of Mr. Gershom Tuttle
Who died Aug 13th AD 1777 in ye 63rd
Year of his age. A man
Of sober life who lived beloved,
Lamented, died & may his rest
With Christ Abide.

In Memory of Mr. John Marshal
Died in this town
Jany [sic] 1, 1802 at 58
On a journey from
Granby Ms. To Landaff NH
In Memory of
Mrs Mary Wife of
Mr Joel Leer &
Daughter of Mr. Meera & Mary Potter
Who died June 17th
1803 aged 26 years 10 months & 25 days
And her infant 6 days buried on her arm.

Here lies the remains
Of Mrs. Nancy Mann
Wife of Lieut Samuel Mann
& Daughter of Capt Reuben Pettys
She died Janry 3rd 1791
In the 26th year of her age
Forbear my friends these drops to shed
And joy to think my woes shall
Cease. Lo, when the valed [sic] Death I tread
I wander from the storm to peace.

In Memory of Mr. William Whiting
Who was killd [sic]
By the fall of a tree
June 2d 1800 aged 38 years.

Mr. Artemas Whiting
Son of Mr. William Whiting &
Mehitable Whiting who has killd
By a fall from a horse
Nov 23, 1799
In the 11th year of his age

Chapter Nine
You Are Not Forgotten

GOODY COLE: HAMPTON

Most New Englanders are familiar with the stories and the sensationalism of the 1692 Salem witchcraft trials. Most people, however, are not aware that town history books throughout the region are filled with stories of lesser-known witches and wizards who are sensational in their own right and who actually pre-date the famous trials. The story of Eunice "Goody" Cole of Hampton is a tale so dramatic and intriguing that it still brings up questions as to whether or not Goody was in fact a witch.

Goody lived on a little hill that overlooked the salt marsh and the Hampton River. She was described as a disagreeable individual and an "unpleasant person." She owned a well that passing boatmen liked to use, much to her dismay. It was said that she wasn't afraid of placing a curse on anyone who she felt had done her wrong in some way. John Greenleaf Whittier's poem "The Wreck of the Rivermouth" describes Goody's curse to a passing mariner:

> *"Fie on the witch!" cried a merry girl,*
> *As they rounded the point where Goody Cole*
> *Sat by her door with her wheel a twirl,*
> *A bent and blear-eyed poor old soul.*
> *"Oho!" she muttered, "ye're brave today!*
> *But I hear the little waves laugh and say,*

The broth will be cold that waits at home;
For it's one to go, but another to come !"
"She's cursed," said the skipper; "speak her fair:
I'm scary always to see her shake
Her wicked head, with its wild gray hair,
And nose like a hawk, and eyes like a snake.
But merrily still, with laugh and shout,
From Hampton River the boat sailed out,
Till the huts and the flakes on Star seemed nigh,
And they lost the scent of the pines of Rye.
They dropped their lines in the lazy tide,
Drawing up haddock and mottled cod;
They saw not the Shadow that walked beside,
They heard not the feet with silence shod.
But thicker and thicker a hot mist grew,
Shot by the lightnings through and through;
And muffled growls, like the growl of a beast,
Ran along the sky from west to east."

According to town history books, Goody was both "hated and feared," and she was considered "aggravating, malicious and revengeful." In 1656, the town's general dislike and suspicion of Goody led to the allegation that she was a witch. Everyone in town seemed to have a story about how Goody had used her evil powers against them. Two young men who drowned in the Hampton River were believed to be victims of her witchcraft. According to her accusers, Goody cast a spell that caused the boat to overturn. The village children who secretly peered into her window described seeing a little black dwarf with a red cap who sat on her table, and when he got out of line, she would "smack his ears." At the trial, Thomas Philbrick testified that Goody cursed his cows; should they eat any of her grass, they would die of poisoning or choke to death.

Goody was found guilty of being familiar with the devil and was sentenced to be publicly whipped. She was then sent to Boston to be imprisoned. In 1662, at the age of eighty-eight, Goody petitioned the court to be released. The court ruled that if she could pay the cost of her board (which was eight pounds per year), she could be released. Goody, however, didn't have the money, so she was not released. After her husband's death, it fell on Hampton's townspeople to pay for Goody's imprisonment. The town stopped paying the bill, and on July 14, 1664, the town selectman was arrested for the balance that was owed. The town turned over the proceeds of her husband's estate, which released them from their debt.

One year later, Goody again petitioned for her release. The court agreed to release on the condition that she move somewhere outside the jurisdiction of the Norfolk court. Goody, however, did not have the means to pay for her transport from Boston. She continued to petition the court in the years that followed, and around 1670, she was returned to Hampton at the town's expense. She was given a small shack to live in, and her neighbors took turns supplying her with meals and firewood. Everyone in town hoped that she would die soon, as they were not interested in doing anything to keep her alive. When she didn't die as quickly as the townspeople had hoped, they raised another charge of witchcraft against her. In 1671, she was indicted by a grand jury in Salisbury; in 1673, after a long trial in Boston, the jury found her not guilty: "In ye case of Unis Cole, now prisoner of ye barr, not legally guilty according to Intitement, butt just ground of vehement suspissyon of her haveing famillarrty with ye devill."

Goody returned to Hampton, but since the town was no longer required to take care of her, she had to fend for herself, and she survived by eating shellfish, roots and berries. The people in town continued to treat her like an outcast and gossiped about her behind her back. Not long after Goody returned, the town noticed her absence, for Goody often walked through town despite being unwelcome. After several days, a group of men visited her old hovel and discovered her dead body lying on a pile of salt marsh hay, which had been her bed. Her body was reportedly thrown in a hole dug by the side of the road, but it wasn't long before it was dug up and impaled on a large stake. (Some say this was done to drive out the devil's spirit, while others say that the act was meant to keep the devil from taking her body to hell).

For years after Goody's death, the townspeople believed that she was behind every tragedy, whether it was a boat that had capsized or an unexplained death. In 1937, an organization called the Society in Hampton for the Apprehension of Those Falsely Accusing Eunice "Goody" Cole of Having Had Familiarity with the Devil was formed. The society lobbied

Judge Perkins to exonerate Goody of all charges of witchcraft and demanded that she be reinstated as a citizen in good standing. On March 8, 1938, on the town's 300th anniversary, a town meeting was held, and the following motion was made and unanimously approved:

> *Resolved: that we, the citizens of the town of Hampton in town meeting assembled do hereby declare that we believe that Eunice (Goody) Cole was unjustly accused of witchcraft and of familiarity with the devil in the seventeenth century, and we do hereby restore that said Eunice (Goody) Cole her rightful place as a citizen of the town of Hampton.*

At two o'clock on August 25 that same year, a crowd gathered at Hampton Beach, along with national news crews, to witness the burning of certified copies of the original incriminating documents. The ashes were placed in a container with soil from both Goody's last home and her final resting place. The urn is now in the Hampton Historical Society's safekeeping.

As part of the town's 300th anniversary, Goody Cole rag dolls were made and sold. An article in the July 7, 1938 edition of the *Hampton Union* described the dolls: "It is expected that many will avail themselves of the opportunity to purchase these dolls as a very striking souvenir of the Tercentenary that Hampton celebrates this year. The doll has the face of a very pleasant elderly lady with movable head, arms and legs and can be completely laundered." There was also a Goody Cole Air Mail postmark that was available at the town post office.

The events and anniversary memorabilia of 1938 were not enough to keep Goody's soul at rest. Many ghost stories continued to circulate throughout Hampton in the following years. Goody's ghost is said to be quiet, and she is reportedly dressed in gray seventeenth-century attire. When this ghost approaches townspeople, she often asks them the whereabouts of some of the original settlers of the town. According to one story from 1955, a Hampton housewife invited a little old woman inside her home for lemonade. Inside, the old woman asked questions regarding the whereabouts of the memorial of Goody Cole and said that she had been searching for it on the Village Green but was unable to find it. When the housewife informed her that there was no such memorial, the old woman stood up and walked out of the house through a closed screen door.

Photograph of the gravestone for Goody Cole, who was convicted of being a witch.

Another story relayed by a police officer told of an old woman walking in the road in the old section of town. The officer stopped her to lecture her about the dangers of walking in the street. The woman replied that she had been walking the streets for hundreds of years and that she should be able to take care of herself by now. The officer started to drive off, but once he realized what she said, he backed his cruiser up to talk to her. The woman, however, had disappeared. Realizing that he had just spoken to a ghost, the officer returned to the station and decided to take a sick day.

It wasn't until 1963 that a memorial gravestone was placed near Founder's Park to help put Goody's soul to rest. The stone, which looks like a woman hunched over, stands on the grounds of the Tuck Museum, which is also the home of the Hampton Historical Society. Many people believe Goody's grave is also on the property, not far from where the monument stands.

There are still reports that Goody's ghost has been sighted near the Tuck Museum, and it is said the she often stands by the memorial stone in quiet reflection. Interestingly enough, there is no carving or indication on the stone that indicates it is a memorial for Goody. Moreover, there are other stones in the area, and unless you know which one you are looking for, you may not recognize it. It might be easier to keep a wary eye out for Goody's ghost. Perhaps she'll show you the way to her memorial stone.

African Burial Ground: Portsmouth

Portsmouth has always been a vibrant city that blends the past with the present. However, in the fall of 2003, while the city was excavating a six-foot hole on Court Street, a coffin was unearthed, and archaeologists were called in to examine it.

Over the course of six days, the coffin and site were examined, and soon, it was determined that there were a total of thirteen bodies in the area. Four of the graves were partially underneath the sidewalk adjacent to Chestnut Street. A hand-dug ditch and nineteenth-century clay sewer pipe were also discovered.

Some of the coffins were well preserved, but most of the remains inside were in a more decayed state. One of the coffins contained a skeleton that was, for the most part, completely intact. However, during the excavation, a backhoe had broken through the coffin and crushed the skull.

After further research, archaeologists found that bodies were the remains of African men and women, and there was even one skeleton that belonged to a child. They also found that this section of Court Street was part of what was once a Negro burial ground that was located just outside the downtown area. The cemetery was in use for nearly one hundred years (starting in 1705), and the last burial, according to records, took place just before 1800. Many of the houses along Court Street were built in the late 1700s and early 1800s, and some were built in the Federalist style (which was popular between the years 1785 and 1815), indicating that the cemetery was hidden and forgotten not long after this last interment. A road connecting the downtown area with the rest of Portsmouth was eventually established over the grounds and paved, erasing all signs that a cemetery had once existed there.

According to record, enslaved blacks arrived in Portsmouth as early as 1645, and there are eleven well-documented slave auctions that took place in the city during the mid- to late 1700s. In addition, the area that was designated for the cemetery in 1705 was listed as a twelve-acre parcel. Many speculate that the remains of at least two hundred people of African descent are interred there, and some historians believe the cemetery may have had as many as three hundred burials. According to several history books, various parts of the cemetery were discovered by accident in the nineteenth and twentieth centuries but were soon lost again. However, there are many people in Portsmouth today who refuse to let history lie underneath the foundations of stately homes.

In November 2008, after much discussion by leading members of the community, a proposal for a monument and spire of remembrance was made. Unfortunately, since it was unknown how deep the bodies were buried and how far the burial ground stretched, city officials decided to conduct an additional survey. Not long after the second dig began, archaeologists discovered more graves just two and a half feet below the street's surface. Coffin and bone fragments were also unearthed, along with a complete skull. The ground was sealed up, and new plans were drafted.

The city decided to build a memorial park on Chestnut Street, but there was one major roadblock: the city did not have enough money. As a result, fundraising programs and events were established, and in June 2012, informational signs were installed in the area, indicating that an African burial ground once stood on the site. The signs offer information about the burial ground, and each is topped with an African sankofa symbol, which looks like a stylized heart and is often associated with the proverb "It is not wrong to go back for that which you have forgotten."

Strangely enough, several houses close to the burial ground are said to be haunted. In fact, the old Parsonage House, built in the mid-eighteenth century, is just down the street, and it is said that one of the rooms in the basement was part of the Underground Railroad. The Sise Inn, which is only a few feet away from the site of the 2003 dig, has two resident ghosts that wander throughout the building. And across the street, there is an old Colonial–style house that is now used as an office condominium. Some have reported seeing lights flickering on and off by themselves and doors locking and unlocking inexplicably.

One thing is for certain: the secrets of the past, although buried for many years, can often resurface to confront the living.

Conclusion

The graveyards and cemeteries of New Hampshire have much to tell to the living about the past. Stories of the humble pioneers who faced the tragic perils of the landscape and those unique individuals whose memory is almost forgotten are buried beneath the rocky soil of the Granite State. The ghosts and spirits who reach out to us from beyond remind us of our own mortality. Can we move past our own superstitions about death and cemeteries and tread the grounds where those who walked the land before us now sleep for all eternity?

Bibliography

Brewster, Charles Warren. *Rambles about Portsmouth: Sketches of Person, Localities, and Incidents of Two Centuries*. Portsmouth, NH: L.W. Brewster Publishing, 1873.

Brighton, Ray. *Frank Jones: King of the Alemakers*. Portsmouth, NH: Peter Randall, 1976.

Citro, Joseph A., and Diane Foulds. *Curious New England: The Unconventional Traveler's Guide to Eccentric Destinations*. Lebanon, NH: UPNE, 2004.

Craig, David V. "The Hampton Witch." *New Hampshire Echoes* 3, no. 6 (January–February 1973).

Cutter, Daniel Bateman. *History of the Town of Jaffrey, New Hampshire, from the Date of the Masonian Charter to the Present Time, 1749–1880*. Concord, NH: Republican Press Association, 1881.

Eastman, John Robie, and George Edwin Emery. *History of the Town of Andover, New Hampshire, 1751–1906*. Concord, NH: Rumford Printing, 1910.

English, Benjamin W. "The Hermit of Crawford Notch." *New Hampshire Echoes* 4, no. 4 (September–October 1973).

Fairfax Downey. *It Happened in New Hampshire*. Grantham, New Hampshire: Thompson & Rutter, 1981.

Friends of the Valley Cemetery. http://friendsofvalleycemetery.com/about-us.

Garvin, James L., and Donna-Belle. "Stephen Webster, Gravestone Maker." *Historical New Hampshire* 24, no. 2 (Summer 1974).

Gore, Moody P., and Guy E. Speare. *New Hampshire Folk Tales, Revised*. Plymouth, NH: self-published, 1945.

Hayward, William Wills. *The History of Hancock, New Hampshire 1764–1889*. Lowell, MA: Vox Populi Press, 1889.

History of Bedford, New Hampshire. Boston: Alfred Mudge, 1851.

Hodgon, George Enos, Thomas W. Hancock and Richard Cutts Shannon. *Reminiscences and Genealogical Record of the Vaughan Family of New Hampshire*. Rochester, NY: Genesee Press, 1918.

Holmes, Rick. "Picket Fence Still Stands Watch Over Lucy's Grave." *Derry News*, May 9, 2012.

Jewett, Jeremiah P. *History of Barnstead [NH] From Its First Settlement, 1727 to 1872*. Lowell, MA: Marden and Rowell, 1872.

Knoblock, Glenn A. *Images of America: Cemeteries Around Lake Winnipesaukee*. Charleston, SC: Arcadia Publishing, 2006.

———. *Images of America: Portsmouth Cemeteries*. Charleston, SC: Arcadia Publishing, 2005.

Merrill, John Leverett. *History of Acworth, New Hampshire*. Springfield, MA: S. Bowles, 1869.

Parker, Edward L. *History of Londonderry, Comprising the Towns of Derry and Londonderry*. Boston: Perkins and Whipple, 1851.

Stepandfetchit, Reuben Y. "Life On The Magalloway." *Granite Monthly* 25 (n.d.).

Waite, Otis F. R. *History of the Town of Claremont.* Manchester, NH: John B. Clarke, 1895.

Washington History Committee. *History of Washington, New Hampshire, from 1768 to 1886.* Claremont, NH: Claremont Manufacturing Company, 1886.

Wetherbee, Fritz. *As Seen on TV.* Concord, NH: Plaidswede, 2010.

———. *Fritz Wetherbee's New Hampshire.* Concord, NH: Plaidswede, 2005.

Whittier, John Greenleaf. *The Poetical Works of John Greenleaf Whittier.* Boston: Houghton Mifflin, 1891.

Varney, Marion L. *Hart's Location in Crawford Notch, New Hampshire's Smallest Town.* Portsmouth, NH: Peter Randall, 1997.

Yates, Elizabeth. "Amos Fortune." *New Hampshire Echoes* 3, no. 6 (January–February 1973).

About the Author

Roxie Zwicker is known for her unique collection of New England folklore and stories. She was born in Boston, Massachusetts, and grew up in New England, surrounded by its beauty and history. After attending Greenfield Community College for Media Production, Roxie found herself exploring the hidden secrets and forgotten history of New England. Since 1993, she has captured audiences with her fascinating storytelling abilities. In 2002, she started her own business called New England Curiosities, giving tours in New Hampshire and Maine that feature many stories from her repertoire. Roxie and New England Curiosities have been featured on the History Channel and the Travel Channel. She has hosted talks on New England legends and lore from New York to Maine and has been featured in over one hundred publications nationwide, including *Better Homes and Gardens*.

Roxie has published six books, many of which are in their second and third printing. She hopes to keep the stories of those who settled in New England alive. For more on Roxie, visit www.RoxieZ.com and www.newenglandcuriosities.com.

Visit us at
www.historypress.net